IMAGES OF WAR

GERMAN ARMY ON THE EASTERN FRONT: THE ADVANCE

RARE PHOTOGRAPHS FROM WARTIME ARCHIVES

Ian Baxter

Pen & Sword
MILITARY

First published in Great Britain in 2015 by
PEN & SWORD MILITARY
An imprint of
Pen & Sword Books Ltd
47 Church Street
Barnsley
South Yorkshire
S70 2AS

ISBN 978-1-47382-266-5

Typeset by Concept, Huddersfield, West Yorkshire HD4 5JL.
Printed and bound in England by CPI Group (UK) Ltd, Croydon CR0 4YY.

Pen & Sword Books Ltd incorporates the imprints of Pen & Sword Archaeology, Atlas, Aviation, Battleground, Discovery, Family History, History, Maritime, Military, Naval, Politics, Railways, Select, Social History, Transport, True Crime, and Claymore Press, Frontline Books, Leo Cooper, Praetorian Press, Remember When, Seaforth Publishing and Wharncliffe.

For a complete list of Pen & Sword titles please contact
PEN & SWORD BOOKS LIMITED
47 Church Street, Barnsley, South Yorkshire, S70 2AS, England
E-mail: enquiries@pen-and-sword.co.uk
Website: www.pen-and-sword.co.uk

Contents

About the Author

Ian Baxter is a military historian who specialises in German twentieth-century military history. He has written more than forty books including *Poland – The Eighteen Day Victory March*, *Panzers in North Africa*, *The Ardennes Offensive*, *The Western Campaign*, *The 12th SS Panzer-Division Hitlerjugend*, *The Waffen-SS on the Western Front*, *The Waffen-SS on the Eastern Front*, *The Red Army at Stalingrad*, *Elite German Forces of World War II*, *Armoured Warfare*, *German Tanks of War*, *Blitzkrieg*, *Panzer-Divisions at War*, *Hitler's Panzers*, *German Armoured Vehicles of World War Two*, *Last Two Years of the Waffen-SS at War*, *German Soldier Uniforms and Insignia*, *German Guns of the Third Reich*, *Defeat to Retreat: The Last Years of the German Army at War 1943–1945*, *Operation Bagration – the destruction of Army Group Centre*, *German Guns of the Third Reich*, *Rommel and the Afrika Korps*, *U-Boat War*, and most recently *The Sixth Army, the Road to Stalingrad*, *German Mountain Troops*, and *Himmler's Nazi Concentration Camp Guards*. He has also written over 100 articles including 'Last Days of Hitler', 'Wolf's Lair', 'Story of the V1 and V2 Rocket Programme', 'Secret Aircraft of World War Two', 'Rommel At Tobruk', 'Hitler's War with his Generals', 'Secret British Plans to Assassinate Hitler', 'SS At Arnhem', 'Hitlerjugend', 'Battle Of Caen 1944', 'Gebirgs-jäger at War', 'Panzer Crews', 'Hitlerjugend Guerrillas', 'Last Battles in the East', 'Battle of Berlin' and many more. He has also reviewed numerous military studies for publication, supplied thousands of photographs and important documents to various publishers and film production companies worldwide, and lectures to various schools, colleges and universities throughout the United Kingdom and Southern Ireland.

Chapter One

Advance to the East

For the invasion of Russia, code-named 'Barbarossa', the German Army assembled some 3 million men, divided into a total of 105 infantry divisions and 32 Panzer divisions. There were 3,332 tanks, over 7,000 artillery pieces, 60,000 motor vehicles and 625,000 horses. This massive force was distributed into three German Army groups:

- *Heeresgruppe Nord* – commanded by *Generalfeldmarschall* Wilhelm Ritter von Leeb, which provided the main spearhead for the advance on Leningrad and assembled in East Prussia on the Lithuanian frontier.
- *Heeresgruppe Mitte* – commanded by *Generalfeldmarschall* Fedor von Bock, which assembled on the 1939 Polish/Russian Frontier, both north and south of Warsaw. Bock's force consisted of forty-two Infantry Divisions of the 4th and 9th Armies, and *Panzergruppen* II and III. This army contained the largest number of German infantry and Panzer divisions in all three army groups.
- *Army Group Süd* – commanded by *Generalfeldmarschall* Gerd von Rundstedt, which was deployed down the longest stretch of border with Russia.

The front, reaching from central Poland to the Black Sea, was held by one *Panzergruppe*, three German and two Rumanian armies, plus a Hungarian motorized corps, under German command.

During the early morning of 22 June 1941, the German Army finally unleashed the maelstrom that was 'Barbarossa'. Both the Infantry and Panzer Divisions wasted no time and soon sliced through the bewildered Russian forces on every front. The ferocity and effectiveness of both the Infantry and Panzer Divisions were so great that groups of up to fifteen Russia divisions were trapped at a time and slowly and systematically annihilated in a hurricane of fire.

In the North, Leeb's rapid two-pronged offensive along the Baltic opened up at first light on the morning of 22 June 1941. His force, consisting of 16th and 18th Armies, smashed through the Soviet defences. Russian soldiers stood helpless in its path, too shocked to take action. Over the next weeks to come, German troops of *Heeresgruppe Nord* continued to chew through enemy positions heading through Lithuania, Latvia and Estonia, straight towards their objective – Leningrad. Fortunately for Leeb, the earth was baked under the blistering summer heat and his army was able to advance rapidly through the Baltic states.

By 10 July, Leeb's units broke south of Pskov and rolled towards Luga. At the rate they were advancing, they would need no more than nine or ten days to reach the outskirts of Leningrad. But following their surge of success, the *Wehrmacht* were losing momentum. Not only were their supply lines being overstretched, but enemy resistance began to stiffen on the road to Leningrad. In a desperate attempt to blunt the German advance and prevent them from reaching the imperial city, brigades of Russian marines, naval units, and more than 80,000 men from the Baltic Fleet were hastily sent into action against Leeb's forces. These Russian soldiers were now the sole barrier between Leningrad and the Germans. Although the advance was hampered by these Russian forces, by the end of August 1941, Leeb's Panzers were finally within sight of Leningrad. The terrified civilians left inside the city walls were now going to endure one of the most brutal sieges in twentieth-century history.

As the summer of 1941 passed and the Germans drew closer to the city gates, Leningraders were given the grim orders to defend their city to the death. Although Leeb's forces had arrived within shelling distance of Leningrad, the advance had not gone as planned. Already units had been badly disrupted and were mired on the Leningrad Front by stiffening resistance.

By 17 September, the Moscow Front could wait no longer for victory in the north. The shift of the main weight, the powerful 41.*Panzerkorps* which Leeb required to sledge-hammer his way to the outskirts of Leningrad, was taken out of line and ordered to the Moscow Front. Without the 41.*Panzerkorps* the whole dynamics of *Heeresgruppe Nord* had altered. There would now be no attack on Leningrad. Instead, Hitler ordered that the city would be encircled and the inhabitants defending inside would be starved to death. During October and November 1941, some ten German divisions were tied down around the city. For the next year German troops of *Heeresgruppe Nord* fought a series of bloody battles to hold their positions around Leningrad. Although they had managed to blunt Russian penetrations through their lines with the sacrifice of thousands of men killed and wounded, the battle had in fact absorbed all the available resources of the 18.Army and elements of the 11.Army, which had resulted in the planned assault on Leningrad being abandoned.

While Leeb's forces smashed their way through Soviet lines during the first promising days of 'Barbarossa', the strongest army group, Army Group Centre, made a series of heavy penetrating drives through the Russian heartlands, bulldozing through the marshy ground to the main Russian defences. Within days of its first attacks across the frontier both the Infantry and Panzer Divisions had pulverized bewildered Russian formations, which led to a string of victories along its entire front.

The ultimate objective of *Heeresgruppe Mitte* was to spearhead as rapidly as possible eastwards to the city of Smolensk, which commanded the road to the Russian capital, Moscow. Facing this impressive array of German might along the River Dnieper and Dvina were groups of heavily defended fortifications called the Stalin Line. The defenders were the Russian 13th Army of the western front, and the 20th Army, 21st Army and the 22nd Army of the Supreme Command (STAVKA) Reserve. In the region around the strategic city of Vitebsk the 19th Army was ordered to hold it at all costs, while the 16th Army was hastily moved in front of Smolensk. It was the threat in the north from 3rd Panzer Army and 39th *Panzerkorps* that seriously worried the Red Army. However, in spite of this concern, Stalin had called for a Great Patriotic War against the Nazi invader, and every soldier was determined to do his duty and hold its lines to grim death. As *Heeresgruppe Mitte* continued a general push towards Smolensk in early July 1941, the Russians began a more determined defence. Many bridges were blown up and, for the first time, the Red Army units began laying mines to slow down the Germans. To make matters worse for both the Infantry and Panzer Divisions heavy rain, typical for July in central Russia, suddenly began turning the roads into streaming rivers of mud, and advancing German units found themselves either slowing down to a painful snail's pace or totally immobile for hours at a time.

The German delays gave the Soviets time to organize for a massive armoured counter-blow.

On 6 July, the Russians finally launched their attack in front of Smolensk with the Soviet 20th Army's 7th and 5th Mechanized Corps attacking advancing German troops and armour with 700 tanks. What followed was the battle of Smolensk with Red Army infantry bitterly contesting every part of ground along the Dnieper River.

To meet the Russian force was Guderian's *Panzergruppe*, which was advancing steadily eastwards, along three separate axes. The most northerly of these ran from the Dnieper crossings below Orsha, along the line Dubrovno-Lyady-Krasny-Smolensk. This was under the 57th *Korps*, with the 29th Motorized Division leading the 17th and 18th Panzer Divisions. In the centre the 56th *Korps* advanced from Mogilev with the 10th Panzer Division, *SS-Das Reich*, and Guard Battalion of *Gross Deutschland*. To the south, up the winding valley of Oster, came the 24th *Korps*, with the 10th Motorized Division, the 3rd and 4th Panzer Divisions, and the cavalry division, all of which were converging toward Smolensk. For the Red Army the Battle of Smolensk would take place in several phases, divided into distinct operations to halt the German offensive and the armoured pincers.

In spite of relatively strong Russian defensive positions, by the second week of July the 3rd *Panzergruppe*'s 20th Panzer Division established a bridgehead on the east bank of the River Dvina and threatened Vitebsk. To the south, away from the main crossings, the 2nd *Panzergruppe* launched surprise attacks, forcing the River Dnieper. The Soviet 13th Army was pushed back, losing five divisions. As both German Panzer Armies drove east, three Soviet Armies, the 20th, 19th and 16th faced the prospect of encirclement around Smolensk.

Meanwhile, south of Smolensk, Guderian's 2nd *Panzergruppe* bulldozed its way through Soviet lines. What followed was intense fighting. Armour and troops from the 29th Motorized Infantry Division in a series of successive attacks blasted their way through towards the city. Soviet soldiers either fought to the death or saved themselves by escaping the impending slaughter by withdrawing to another makeshift position. During the early morning of 16 July fighting intensified with even greater losses to the Russians. The battles that took place in and around Smolensk became a fierce contest of attrition, and although the Russians showed great fortitude and determination, they were constantly hampered by lack of the weapons and man-power needed to sustain them on the battlefield. Consequently, the remaining troops holding out in the city were subjected to merciless ground and aerial bom-bardments. The situation for the defenders looked grim. The ferocity of the German attack was relentless. After nearly twenty-four hours of almost continuous battle the Russian soldiers had become exhausted. Stalin's insistence that his troops must fight from fixed positions without any tactical retreat had caused many units to become encircled, leaving tank units to speed past unhindered and achieve even deeper penetrations.

By the early afternoon of 16 July Smolensk was finally captured by 29th Motorized Infantry Division. In the north, Hoth's 3rd *Panzergruppe* was moving much more slowly. The terrain was swampy and the rain was still hampering operations in a number of places. The Russians were fighting desperately to escape the trap that was developing. On 18 July, the great armoured pincers of the two German Panzer Armies came within ten miles of closing the gap. But the jaws would not finally snap shut, and bitter fighting raged for more than a week.

While the battle of Smolensk raged and the Germans tried liquidating the Smolensk pocket; with some 500,000 Soviet troops fighting inside, General Guderain immediately set about implementing plans to crush Soviet forces further east around the town of Roslavl. The operation had taken the Red Army completely by surprise. The sudden speed and depth of the German attack was a brilliant display of all-arms coordination. In some areas along the front, units were easily brushed aside and totally destroyed. Red Army survivors recalled that they had been caught off-guard, having been lulled into a false sense of security after escaping from the Smolensk pocket. Now they were being attacked by highly mobile armour and blasted by heavy artillery. In many places the force of the attack was so heavy that they were unable to organize any type of defence. In total confusion, hundreds of troops, disheartened and frightened, retreated to avoid the slaughter, while other more fanatical units remained, ruthlessly defending their positions to the death. On 1 August, Guderian launched his Roslavl offensive. The Russian force that was thrown into the German attack consisted of remnants from the battle of Smolensk. They were exhausted, short of ammunition and vulnerable. On the right wing of the German attack stood the 4th Panzer Division which broke into open country within a few hours and ripped across the Russian front. The armoured division, with infantry trailing to the rear, advanced nearly thirty miles, and by evening of 2 August was outside the town of Roslavl. The 29th Motorized Division had meanwhile pushed steadily down the valley of the Desna. The Russians tried desperately to hold onto the town of Roslavl, but under direct attack by seven fresh German infantry divisions, the defence soon crumbled away. Around the town a pocket soon began to form, with Germans bringing up greater artillery concentration, while Red Army troops feebly tried to break out. Roslavl finally fell to the Germans on 3 August. Guderian order a Panzer striking force of three divisions immediately ordered away from the main battle to probe southwards and clear up stragglers from both Smolensk and Roslavl.

The battles of Smolensk and Roslavl were two of the swiftest and most complete German Army victories in the East. Altogether some 300,000 Soviet soldiers had been captured in the Smolensk pocket. However 200,000 had managed to break out and fight in Roslavl and surrounding areas further east. The Red Army troops left from both battles were used to stand between the Germans and Moscow, as *Heeresgruppe Mitte* desperately tried to reach the Russian capital before winter.

A column of vehicles has halted on a road near the Soviet frontier. The soldiers wear the standard pattern army field-grey greatcoat with field-grey collar. The greatcoat has been correctly worn buttoned up to the neck, with the collar being worn turned up around the wearer's neck and lower part of the face. A small cloth flap was buttoned across the throat and attached to a small button on the opposite side of the coat.

Here two soldiers sleep during the long journey through Russia. The soldier on the right is wearing a medical personnel badge – a yellow serpent and staff on a dark green circular background. In order to distinguish those German troops who undertook various military functions and who had achieved a specialist trade, special badges were introduced.

(*Opposite page*) Two soldiers at a lookout post peer through 6 × 30 Sf.14Z scissor binoculars, which were nicknamed by the troops as 'donkey ears'. The soldier looking through the binoculars holds the rank of *Obergefreiter*, while the man standing next to him holds the rank of Lieutenant. Note he has a microphone in his hand, which suggests he is a war correspondent recording frontline propaganda for the radio.

During a ceremony two Panzer crewman can be seen standing in front of a Pz.Kpfw.I with the national flag draped over the tank's frontal armour. Both Panzer men wear the famous black Panzer uniform with Panzer beret. This special Panzer uniform consisted of a short black double-breasted jacket worn with long black trousers. The uniform was the same design and colouring worn for all ranks of the Panzer arm.

A soldier examines a machine gun with another man. On the lower right sleeve he is wearing a badge indicating he is a Motor Transport NCO. The Gothic 'S' is in yellow on a dark blue-green circular background. Virtually all German Army trade and specialist badges were manufactured in yellow cotton or silk thread on a circular or oval backing.

(*Opposite page*) *Gebirgsjäger* troops march across a pontoon bridge that has been heavily camouflaged with foliage. The *Gebirgsjäger* were primarily trained to ski, climb and endure long marches, survive appalling conditions and were given a role as crack shock troops. Yet many campaigns in which the *Gebirgsjäger* fought were on level ground where they had little opportunity to demonstrate their unique skills. The *Gebirgsjäger* wore the same style German Army service uniform except that the field service jacket displayed the edelweiss arm badge on the upper right sleeve and the headdress, normally the *Bergmütze*, would be that used by army mountain troop formations.

A group of soldiers rest during the early part of the war. The photograph is an excellent display of an infantryman's personal equipment. Secured on the soldier's back is a web pack carrier that is attached to his support Y-straps, to which his mess kit and Zeltbahn are attached. The canteen tin is attached to the bread bag, which carried rations as well as other items. The gas mask canister can be seen attached at the bottom of the kit. All of the soldiers are wearing the M1938 field cap and standard issue M1936 field service tunic.

Four of the five man crew of a Pz.Kpfw.IV can be seen moving along a road in the early summer of 1941 on the Eastern Front. They all wear the black Panzer uniform and M1938 black Panzer field cap. The Panzer jacket was specially designed, like the trousers, to allow the wearer plenty of movement inside the cramped confines of an armoured vehicle. With no external pockets this also minimized any jacket snagging on protruding parts of the tank.

A German soldier with his German Shepherd dog. The soldier is wearing an M1936 service uniform. The German national emblem of an eagle with outstretched wings clutching in its claws a wreath containing a swastika can be seen positioned on the right breast of the service tunic. The uniform had four box-pleated patch pockets; five field-grey finished metal buttons were positioned down the front of the tunic, with another button to each of the four pockets. The style of pockets was a design adopted from the Austro-Hungarian Army tunic worn during the First World War.

While buildings have been set ablaze by artillery, soldiers of the *Gebirgsjäger* march along a road in 1941. Although trained as mountain troops these elite bands of men were invariably employed as assault infantry in conventional battle, a role in which every individual *Gebirgsjäger* trooper excelled, but not the one for which they had been trained. The mountain troops fought in virtually all theatres of the Second World War, especially on the Eastern Front, where operations took them into the Caucasus. The *Gebirgsjäger* were proud to accept the harsh conditions because they wore the edelweiss, the famous badge that set them apart and distinguished them as Hitler's mountain troops.

Soldiers are marching along a road during the opening phase of the invasion of Russia. In this photograph it shows some of the personal equipment worn by the German Army during this period of the war. One soldier can be seen wearing some of his kit on his back, which includes the mess tin, Zeltbahn cape and bread bag. The M1935 helmet can be seen attached strapped around the mess tin for ease of carriage. Note the near soldier with his M1938 field cap stuffed through his infantryman's leather belt.

Signal operators jot down messages that they have received. The soldier on the right who holds the rank of *Gefreiter* wears on his upper left sleeve a signal-operators badge that consisted of a lightning 'Blitz' in yellow on a dark blue-green oval background. Other colours too were also worn with this badge, which included sometimes pink or white.

Once German forces had occupied areas of the Soviet Union, various administrative organizations were moved in to the particular occupied zone of operations; these included Military Policemen or *Feldgendarmerie*. In this photograph German Military Police are questioning Russian peasants. They wear the standard German Army M1936 service uniform with the dull aluminum Gorget plate suspended around the neck by a chain.

German troops on the Eastern Front in the summer of 1941 march along a road. All the soldiers wear a host of personal equipment that is worn with the M1936 field service uniform. The sleeves of the tunic have been rolled up because of the daytime temperatures, which were often very warm, especially in southern Russia. The company commanders at the front hold the ranks of *Oberleutnant* and *Oberfeldwebel*.

A Flak gun mounted on a halftrack. Foliage has been applied to the vehicle in order to minimise the possibility of aerial detection. All the soldiers are wearing the standard army M1936 service uniform and M1935 steel helmet. What the soldiers are wearing suggests that this photograph was taken during the summer months of 1941.

(*Opposite above*) An interesting photograph showing what appears to be non-German troops in *Wehrmacht* uniforms on the Eastern Front. Not all these soldiers wore their grey braid chevrons, but this unit is unique as it shows almost every man holding the ranks of *Gefreiter* or *Obergefreiter*. The chevrons was a rank system used throughout the German Army and was designed to show the wearer's rank on the upper left arm of the uniform tunic, the service and field service tunics, and the greatcoat.

(*Opposite below*) The distances that were travelled on foot across Russia were often immense. Here in this photograph are three soldiers that have commandeered a child's pram in order to transport spare clothing and personal equipment including their M1935 steel helmets. The canvas satchel-like bags are used to carry clothing. All three soldiers wear the M1936 service uniform along with the standard black leather marching boots. The trousers have been tucked into the boots, which was normally standard practice in the German Army. Note the top collars of the soldier's tunics, which have been unbuttoned in order to try and keep them relatively cool.

A German officer and motorcyclist survey a map during operations during 1941. The motorcyclist is wearing a greatcoat with his personal equipment. The gas mask canister can be seen slung around on his chest, which was a common place for motorcyclists to wear them. The advance through Russia was often perilous, especially for wheeled vehicles, which frequently became stuck along muddy roads. The road system too sometimes caused problems that often resulted in traffic congestion.

A machine gun crew rest during operations in Russia in 1941. They are wearing a variety of personal equipment, which includes the M1939 infantry leather support straps, rifle ammunition pouches, bread bag and gas mask canister. For the German soldier fighting in the summer of 1941 the success of the summer months led to many believing the war would soon be won. However, the Soviet Union proved to be a completely alien environment to the German soldier, and the distances travelled soon proved more of a problem than ever imagined. Russia would not only test the endurance of the German soldier's physical stamina, but also his weapons and supplies.

An *Unteroffizier* searches for enemy armour and uses the tyre of a camouflaged 3.7cm Pak 36 to steady his right arm as he looks through his binoculars. He wears the M1936 service uniform worn under battlefield conditions. On his tunic pinned to his left pleated box-pocket is the Knights Cross decoration of second-class grade and a military decoration badge awarded to troops for their individual skill at arms under battlefield conditions.

An unusual photograph showing Panzer crews washing their Pz.Kpfw.IV tanks in a river. A number of the men appear to be wearing the reed-green two-piece Panzer denim suit, which was a hardwearing light and easy washable garment. It was identical in cut to the special black Panzer uniform and was intended to be used during the summer months. It was also used as an outer garment over the black Panzer uniform. The normal insignia and national emblem was worn with this two-piece Panzer denim suit.

(*Opposite page*) A German soldier armed with a flamethrower 35. This weapon contained a compressed nitrogen propellant. The soldier holds the rank of *Gefreiter* as indicated by the chevron stitched onto his upper left arm. The chevron was made from 0.9cm wide braiding dull grey or bright silver depending on the type of uniform being worn at the time.

A soldier on the Eastern front in the summer of 1941. The soldier is wearing his M1935 steel helmet, which has been smeared with mud in order to reduce the reflective shine and increase camouflage protection. This rifleman has been issued with a field flashlight. Secured in his infantryman's leather belt is an Stg24 stick hand grenade, which was commonly known in the German Army as the 'Potato masher'. The hand grenade became a widely used weapon in the German Army and popular throughout the war.

Troops wearing their distinctive M1936 service uniform and steel helmets have rounded up local male civilians during the invasion of the Soviet Union. German forces often recruited Russian volunteers for supplementary service in a number of roles including cooks, ammunition carriers, messengers and drivers.

A soldier wearing the early style greatcoat with M1935 steel helmet. He is preparing a concentration charge, which was primarily used as an anti-tank weapon or for knocking out bunkers. The charge was made by securing six stick grenade heads with detonators removed around the central stick grenade. The weapon was very effective and could cause a tremendous blast.

Troops pass through a village. One soldier can be seen holding an MG 34 machine gun slung over his shoulder for ease of carriage. The MG 34 weighed 25.4 pounds and was considered one of the best machine guns of the Second World War. Personal equipment on the MG 34 squad appears to be limited. A mess tin can be seen attached to the MG 34 machine gunner's leather belt.

(*Opposite above*) A convoy of Pz.Kpfw.38(t) roll along a road. Allowing the tanks to pass and continue their spearhead is a column of horse-drawn transport parked along side of the road. On the opposite side of the road is a stationary motorcyclist dressed in his standard army field service uniform. The crew on board the tanks are wearing their familiar special black Panzer uniforms with M1938 black caps. The special black Panzer uniform was the same design and colouring for all ranks of the Panzer arm including Generals of the *Panzertruppen*.

(*Opposite below*) Two soldiers holding the rank of *Gefreiter* sit on a cannibalised motorcycle combination. The hand-painted 'WL' on the sidecar indicates that the vehicle belonged at some point to the '*Wehrmacht Luftwaffe*'. A *Gefreiter* was the German equivalent of Private in the German Army and was the lowest rank to which an ordinary soldier could be promoted.

During the first victorious months of operations in the Soviet Union the German Army rounded up millions of Russian soldiers. Here in this photograph captured Soviet prisoners are frisked for hidden weapons. The German soldiers are wearing a variety of personal equipment including the trademark M1935 steel helmet. Also worn are the combat harness for the mess kit and the Zeltbahn, an entrenching tool carrier, bread bag for rations, and a gas mask canister with anti-gas cape in its pouch attached to the shoulder strap. The soldier on the left is armed with a 7.92mm Kar 98k bolt action Mauser rifle, which was the standard German rifle.

(*Opposite above*) A column of Panzers from the 18th Panzer Division moves along a dusty road in Russia. The 18th Panzer Division was formed in October 1940 and saw extensive action on the Russian central and southern fronts between 1941 and 1943. The Panzer crew are not wearing their black Panzer jackets, only the dark grey tricot shirt without pockets. The Panzer shirt had a four-button front and buttons and loops for the attachment of shoulder boards or shoulder straps. Wearing just the shirt was common among crews when daytime temperatures were high.

(*Opposite below*) The crew of a Pz.Kpfw.IV are on board their stationary vehicle in Russia during the summer of 1941. This vehicle was part of the 1st Panzer Division, which operated on both the northern and central fronts between 1941 and 1943. The crew are all wearing the black Panzer uniform. Although the uniforms could easily hide oil and grease stains it was soon realised in Russia that they were not practical enough when a crewman left the vehicle in the field, as the garment stood out.

A soldier is armed with the popular 9mm MP 38/40 machine pistol. This weapon was used throughout the campaign on the Eastern Front and was commonly nicknamed by the troops, the 'Schmeisser'. This particular machine pistol the soldier is carrying has seven 32-round magazines — one on the weapon and three spares in each of his two magazine pouches. He is also well armed with Stg24 stick hand grenades, which have been secured in his black leather service uniform belt.

Two German officers on the Eastern Front in 1941. Both are wearing the gas cape pouch worn on the web strap of the gas mask canister. These early pouches were made from rubberized canvas. The soldier on the left has been issued with 6 × 30 binoculars. One of the most common ways of securing binoculars to prevent them from bouncing and swinging was to secure them to a tunic button. Neither soldier carries magazine pouches. Note the horse in the background, which has the M1935 steel helmet attached to the saddle.

An injured soldier is helped through a Russian village by his comrade during summer operations in 1942. They have been issued with the standard M1936 field blouse with its typical dark green facing collar, decorative army collar M1938, Litzen insignia, and plain dark shoulder straps with white colour piping to indicate infantry. In 1940, shoulder straps were no longer manufactured without regimental numbers.

(*Opposite above*) The crew of a Pz.Kpfw.III can be seen on board their armoured vehicle prior to its departure by train to the Eastern Front. Foliage has been applied to parts of the Panzer in order to reduce the risk of aerial detection. Three of the five-man crew are wearing the standard black Panzer uniform, while the other two crew members are wearing the tricot shirt.

(*Opposite below*) German rifle troops wearing a host of personal equipment march across a pontoon bridge in 1941. Attached to the support straps they are wearing the gas mask canister, canteen, bread bag, and ammunition pouches, and attached to the small backpack is the M1935 steel helmet. The backpack provided the soldier with spare clothing, personal items, and additional rations, along with a satchel-like spare clothing bag. These backpacks were typically carried in the rifle platoons. All the soldiers are armed the 7.92mm Kar Mauser bolt-action rifle.

General Heinz Guderian conferring with other high-ranking officers. All the men wear the finely woven gold cording braid shoulder straps and fine gold embroidered collar patches, which indicate they hold the rank of General.

General Heinz Guderian is standing next to an Sd.Kfz.251 halftrack in the summer of 1941. He wears shoulder and collar patches that indicate he holds the rank of General. The shoulder straps have finely woven gold cording braid on either side of a single strand of silver strap to show four loop holes of braid on each side of the strap. As for the collar patches these are very elaborate in design and were made in fine gold embroidery on a dark green backing material piped in the appropriate red *Waffenfarbe*.

This photograph was more than likely taken at General Heinz Guderian's mobile field headquarters in the summer of 1941. It shows an officer and a General scrutinizing a situation map. Both men are wearing breeches with their tunic and high leather riding boots. The General is a holder of the Knight's Cross first class and can be seen wearing it around his neck.

An infantryman with foliage attached to his M1935 steel helmet surveys the terrain ahead through his 6 × 30 binoculars. Apart from the standard M1936 service uniform for this period of the war, he has been issued with the usual equipment and weapons of an infantryman. He wears the M1939 infantry leather support straps, two-rifle ammunition pouches, and has two M1924 stick grenades secured into his belt.

(*Opposite above*) General Heinz Guderian confers with one of his divisional commanders. Both men wear the general's field-grey greatcoat. The design and cut was identical to the greatcoat worn by all ranks, however the quality was usually produced to a very high standard. The greatcoats have a dark blue-green collar, which when worn open revealed the red-faced lapels. The buttons on the garment were of gilt coloured metal and the shoulder straps were always worn displaying the wearer's rank. The inside of the coat above the waist was lined in bright red.

(*Opposite below*) Two Generals in a rather relaxed scene can be seen conferring with the aid of maps regarding the next operational move on the German Central Front in the summer of 1941. Both generals wear the woven gold cording braid shoulder straps and gold embroidered collar patches.

A machine gun team are commandeering transport to move their MG 34 machine gun and two ammunition cases along a road in Russia in the summer of 1941. It was common practice for troops to utilise various modes of transport, especially with heavier equipment. The soldier on the left can clearly be seen wearing a rank chevron positioned on his left upper arm indicating that he holds the rank of *Obergefreiter*.

Two fully equipped MG 34 machine gunners in a field in Russia during operations in 1942. Both men hold the rank of *Gefreiter*, as indicated by their chevrons. The backing cloth on the chevrons normally varied in colour depending on the type of uniform being worn. However, with the standard issue German service uniform they were dark blue-green material or field-grey. In this photograph the soldier on the left has field-grey backing cloth, while his comrade has dark blue-green.

In the summer of 1941, four of the five-man crew of a Pz.Kpfw.IV are seen moving along a road. The Pz.Kpfw.IV vehicle became the most popular and liked Panzer of the Second World War, and remained in production throughout the war. At first it was not intended to be the main armoured vehicle of the Panzerwaffe, but it soon proved to be so diverse and effective that it became the most widely used of all main battle tanks during the conflict.

On the Russian southern front in the summer of 1941, a local peasant gives an *Unteroffizier* a lift aboard his horse-drawn cart. The group leader wears an M1938 field cap with his standard army service uniform, which suggests that it is not in battlefield conditions. His kit and weapons are more than likely inside the cart. During this period of the war, Ukrainian nationalists were recruited from ex-soldiers in order to aid and support the German drive southeast, and this included transporting supplies and troops across the vast expanses of the Ukraine.

A two-man mortar crew wearing the M1938 field cap. This suggests that these soldiers are not fighting under battle conditions, but more than likely on a training exercise, in the late summer of 1940. Both the soldiers wear the familiar standard issue army uniform for this period of the war and are equipped with the web battle pack carrier fastened to the back of their support straps to carry their mess kit, shelter cape, and other important gear to sustain them on the battlefield.

An MG 34 machine gun team on the eastern front in 1941. The soldiers all wear the M1936 service uniform. The gunner on the left holding the MG 34 machine gun holds the rank of *Oberschütze*, which is identified by the four-pointed star on a circular backing on his left arm. The soldier to his left, known as his number two, carries two ammunition boxes, while the number three carries the spare barrels and another ammunition case.

A German unit rests by the side of a road on the Eastern Front during the summer of 1941. With the campaign in Russia thought to be more or less won, there was a widespread feeling of ease within the ranks of the invaders. A multitude of standard infantry equipment and weapons are being carried. Within four months of the initial success of the campaign in the East, German soldiers would be freezing in their service uniforms, the only thing keeping them warm being the standard army issue greatcoat.

(*Opposite above*) A motorcyclist has incurred a mechanical defect with his machine, probably due to the extreme muddy conditions. The mud produced from a few hours of rain in Russia was enough to immobilize whole columns of wheeled transport, even tanks. The motorcyclist is wearing the standard waterproof coat, which has a collar faced in field-grey wool and two large pockets in the front and side, each with a large button-down pocket flap. He is armed with a 7.92mm Kar 98k Mauser bolt-action rifle.

(*Opposite below*) There were more than 800,000 horses on the Eastern Front in 1941, and by the time the winter arrived some 8,000 of them a day were being killed by enemy fire, by the extreme arctic temperatures, or from over-exertion. Here a group of soldiers tend to a horse that has clearly over-exerted itself by trying to pull a cart through the snow and mud. As for the clothing of the troops, the majority are wearing the standard pattern army field-grey greatcoat with dark blue-green collar. An officer is also wearing the army pattern field-grey greatcoat, which is identical to those worn by other ranks except for the reinforced leather patches to the shoulders indicating his rank, and the officer's field cap.

A Panzer commander standing inside the cupola of a Pz.Kpfw.III while serving on the Eastern Front during the first winter period. The uniform shows the standard black Panzer uniform with the newly introduced Panzer enlisted man's field cap. The commander can clearly be seen wearing the tank crew headset, which was worn in conjunction with a throat microphone. These were essential pieces of kit if the crew were to hear orders from the commander over the noise of the tank's engines.

(*Opposite above*) The early style greatcoat was the most common winter garment issued during the first winter period of the war in Russia. This pre-war greatcoat was a double-breasted garment made of high quality woollen cloth. The colour was a greenish shade of field grey. It had two rows of buttons and two slanted hip pockets with rounded flaps. Under the greatcoat they are more than likely wearing the M1936 field service uniform tucked into the traditional long shaft leather marching boots. Their winter clothing consists of woollen toques under the M1935 steel helmet with thick woollen gloves. Worn over the greatcoat is the usual rifleman's equipment and weapons including the leather belt and ammunition pouches.

(*Opposite below*) On a mountainside these troops, more than likely part of the mountain troops or *Gebirgsjäger*, rest during operations in Russia in 1941. All the soldiers are wearing the German Army field-grey greatcoat. This standard pattern greatcoat with its dark blue-green collar can be seen worn with personal equipment. One of the soldiers is armed with a stick grenade, which is secured in his infantryman's leather belt. An MG 34 machine gun can also be seen.

A crewmember of a Pz.Kpfw.IV is loading ammunition through the tank's hatch. The crewmember is wearing the black Panzer uniform with black M1938 field cap and in order to keep him warm he is wearing an animal skin fur coat. The arms of the garment have been purposely removed in order to allow the wearer more movement inside the cramped confines of the tank. The use of such additional wear over the black Panzer uniform during this period of the war was not common, and by the later stages it became more frequent, especially with the increasing need for additional warmth and camouflage.

A group of troops on the Eastern Front in the first winter period in Russia in late 1941. They all wear the standard pattern army field-grey greatcoat with dark blue-green collar worn with a woollen toque, mittens, and M1938 field cap. This particular style of army greatcoat was normal issue throughout the *Reichsheer* and was issued during the early war years until stocks became exhausted.

German soldiers on the Eastern Front probably in late 1941, early 1942. Here all the troops wear another form of winter camouflage, the snow overall. This white garment was an early piece of snow clothing. It was long, which covered the entire service uniform and was designed to reach the wearer's ankles. It was shapeless, had buttons right down the front, had a deep collar, and had an attached hood and long sleeves. The black infantryman's leather belt and personal equipment was worn attached around the outside of the garment in order to allow better access.

An interesting photograph showing troops marching through the snow in late 1941 wearing a variety of early winter camouflage garments. The soldier leading the march is wearing a white cotton blanket crudely tied around his tunic. This was an early attempt by troops at snow camouflage. Behind the soldier the men wear a mixture of camouflage clothing including the two-piece snowsuit, snow shirts, and snow overalls.

An MG 34 machine gun squad wearing the snow overalls tuck into some rations during a lull in the fighting in Russia. The headdress they are wearing was all part of the winter uniform. This consisted of the helmet toque and tight fitting hoods. The close fitting headdress was primarily designed for warmth and was made of either woollen or cloth material.

(*Opposite page*) Freezing German troops are attempting to protect themselves from the snow with their Zeltbahn. The Zeltbahn was not considered a winter garment and although it protected the wearer from snow showers, it certainly did not provide adequate protection from the sub-zero temperatures in Russia. It appears that these soldiers are not wearing their standard issue greatcoats.

The first winter period on the Eastern Front in late 1941, and troops use draught animals to pull sledges along a road during Army Group Centre's drive on Moscow. The soldiers are wearing the German Army standard issue great-coat with toque and M1938 field cap. The German Army lacked sufficient provisions to sustain their force during a winter war and as a consequence many thousands got frostbite and other ailments caused by the extreme sub-zero temperatures.

(*Opposite above*) Two soldiers tucking into their rations are wearing the reversible snow suit on the Eastern Front in 1943. The man on the left, wearing his M1935 camouflaged steel helmet, has his padded winter garment white side out, while his comrade, wearing an M1938 field cap with toque, has it grey side out. The reversible grey side was officially manu2factured in reed green; however factories seem to have produced them in a darker steel grey colour.

(*Opposite below*) A soldier wearing a two-piece snow camouflage suit. He wears a coloured armband on his left arm, which enabled German troops to distinguish between friend and foe. Generally the colour armband was green but it could be changed in colour or position depending on the frequently changing security sequence.

Two soldiers, more than likely on guard duties, during operations on the Eastern Front in 1941. Both troops wear the standard army field greatcoat with woollen toque beneath their M1938 field cap. Scarves were sometimes worn with the toque in order to help provide the wearer with extra insulation. The first winter period in Russia was a severe ordeal for the German Army and paralysed the German drive on Moscow (code-named Operation 'Typhoon').

(*Opposite above*) The crew of a StuG.III of *Sturmartillerie Abteilung* 197 on the Eastern Front in the winter of 1941. Three of the crewmembers wear the standard field-grey *Sturmartillerie* uniform with Death's Head emblems, while one of them can be seen dressed in the standard army greatcoat. All of them wear the M1938 grey field cap, which was a typical form of *Sturmartillerie* dress for this early period of the war.

(*Opposite below*) Here German soldiers march towards the front during the winter of 1941. All the men wear the toque, which was a sleeve-like wool tube that was designed to be pulled over the head to protect the wearer's neck and parts of the face from the bitter cold. Occasionally two or even three toques were worn for extra insulation along with scarves.

An MG 34 machine gun crew rest during a lull in the fighting on the Eastern Front in 1943. Three of the MG squad are wearing toques beneath their M1935 steel helmets. The soldier sitting between both gunners carries the weapons tripod. A typical infantry battalion's machine gun company had three platoons of heavy machine guns each, which were considered more than enough for both offensive and defensive actions.

Chapter Two

Army Group South 1942

By the spring of 1942 Hitler, who was now in full command of the *Wehrmacht*, was determined to smash the Red Army once and for all in southern Russia. An ambitious plan was worked out that involved the seizure of Stalingrad, and the isthmus between the Don and the Volga. Following the capture of the city of Stalingrad he planned using the city as an anchor from which to send the mass of his panzer force south to occupy the Caucasus, where it would be used to cut off vital Russian oil supplies. The operation was called Operation 'Blau'. The directive that Hitler himself dictated was executed in two stages. The first part of the summer operation was a determined all-out drive in successive enveloping thrusts along the Kursk-Voronezh axis, where it was to destroy the Soviet southern flank and carry on to the Don River. The second part was the advance to Stalingrad and across the lower Don into the Caucasus. For this operation *Heeresgruppe Süd* would be divided. He ordered General List's *Heeresgruppe* A south towards Rostov and the Caucasus, while General Weichs's *Heeresgruppe* B would be responsible for the drive across the lower Don to the Volga and into Stalingrad.

In the regroup, *Heeresgruppe* B took command of the 2nd, 4th, and 6th Armies, the first two being detached from *Heeresgruppe Mitte*. *Heeresgruppe* A was assigned with the 1st, 11th, and 17th Armies. In order to support the drive to the Volga, Italy, Hungary and Rumania took to the field. Though these allied forces were under-equipped and badly trained, they were nonetheless helpful in bolstering the German forces in the area. For the summer offensive a number of divisions, especially those spearheading the drive were brought to authorized strength levels and included artillery, and anti-tank and anti-aircraft weapons. German strength in the air was equal to that of the 1941 campaign with 1,500 aircraft of the total 2,750 being sent down to the southern sector of the front.

As they stood poised to unleash their forces through southern Russia to the western banks of the Volga, it seemed that the Germans now held the upper hand. At dawn on 28 June 1942, the 2nd and 4th Panzer Armies opened up the 'Blau' offensive. Almost immediately the panzers smashed their way through lines of Red

Army defences and drove at breakneck speed east of Kursk and pushed toward Voronezh, reaching the outskirts of the smouldering city in four days. Following the capture of the city, 4th Panzer Division then swung southeast along the Don where it met with Paulus' 6th Army east of Kharkov. Over the next few weeks, strung out over more than 200 miles 6th Army with twenty divisions (250,000 men, 500 panzers, 7,000 guns and mortars, and 25,000 horses) pushed down towards the Don corridor on Stalingrad. The tremendous distances which these divisions had to cover could only be achieved by long foot-marches. Due to the lack of adequate rail and road links, natural obstacles such as the *balka*, which were high, steep-sided, dried-up watercourses, often obstructed the advance of a tank column until a diversion was made or a bridge erected. In some areas of the advance it was hampered by the lack of fuel, which had been temporarily diverted to *Heeresgruppe* A, because it had been ordered to thrust into the Caucasus and capture Grozny and the Baku oilfields. The 1st Panzer Army spearheaded the attack. Initially successful attacks were led, with Rostov, Maikop, Krasnodar, and the entire Kuban region captured. But in a number of areas there was bitter opposition and the Russians managed to hold large parts of the front. Though Russian resistance was sometimes patchy and disorganized, again and again their units fought superbly and to the death. Once more German troops found themselves unexpectedly heavily engaged. Tormented by stiff opposition some units were barely able to maintain cohesion, and were soon repulsed by skilfully deployed Russian soldiers. All along the German front to the east erupted into flame. A number of areas were ablaze as artillery, mortars, and tanks unleashed their firepower. Across selected terrain, panzers led across open fields. As they approached enemy emplacements they allowed the infantry to overtake them and sweep in against anti-tank guns, before the tanks themselves once again took over. The Russians had once more proved to be fearless defenders and this was particularly true of the anti-tank gun crews that played a key role in combating German armour.

By September 1942, despite heavy and unrelenting engagements, the *Heeresgruppe* A offensive was stalled in the Caucasus, and List was relieved of his command. After Hitler briefly took personal control of *Heeresgruppe* A, on 21 November 1942, he appointed von Kleist to personally take command. While von Kleist got himself acquainted with his new command, *Heeresgruppe* Don was created from the headquarters of the 11th Army in the southern sector of the Eastern Front on 22 November. The army group only lasted until February 1943 when it was combined with *Heeresgruppe* B and was made into the new *Heeresgruppe Süd*. The commander of *Heeresgruppe* Don was *Generalfeldmarschal* Erich von Manstein. At the same time General Eberhard von Mackensen was placed in charge of the 1st Panzer Army.

Heeresgruppe Don's task was to bring the enemy attacks to a standstill and re-capture the positions previously occupied by German forces. However, the situation in the area was less favourable for the Germans, for they were pitting their strength against much larger and better equipped enemy formations. Manstein's *Heeresgruppe* Don initially consisted of the 6th Army, which was surrounded at Stalingrad by an enemy three times as strong. It was also composed of remnants of the once highly regarded 4th Panzer Army and two Rumanian armies. The best force that Manstein possessed was the intact 16th Motorized Division and four Rumanian divisions. To raise more forces needed to sustain itself on the battlefield Manstein knew it was imperative to shift certain formations from *Heeresgruppe* A and allot them to his Don force. The *Feldmarschal* was also aware of the dire situation of the 6th Army at Stalingrad and wanted to send a relief force to the beleaguered soldiers now trapped in and around the city.

By December 1942 the 6th Army became increasingly embroiled in bitter and bloody urbanized fighting inside the ruined city of Stalingrad. Operation 'Winter Storm' was launched on 12 December in an attempt to relieve the trapped 6th Army at Stalingrad. The attack was spearheaded by General Kirchner's LVII *Panzerkorps*, consisting of the 6th Panzer Division, which was bolstered by some 160 tanks and forty self-propelled guns, and the mauled 23rd Panzer Division. Protecting the *Panzerkorps*' flanks were Rumanian troops and two weak cavalry divisions. During the first few uneasy days of the attack the panzers steadily rolled forward, making good progress over the light snow. But despite this auspicious beginning Manstein's forces were up against strong resilient opponents. On the second day of the operation the LVII *Panzerkorps* reached the Aksay River and captured the bridge at Zalivskiy. With heavy *Luftwaffe* support the advance moved progressively, but Manstein's forces still had another forty-five miles to cover before it reached the pocket. On 17 December the LVII *Panzerkorps* increased to three divisions due to the arrival of the 17th Panzer Division. With this added strength Kirchner pushed his forces hard across the snow, fighting bitterly as they advanced. Around the town of Kumsky, halfway between the Aksay and Mishkova Rivers, the corps became bogged down in a morass of heavy protracted fighting against two strong Russian mechanized corps and two tank brigades. It seemed that Manstein's fervent attempt to reach the Kessel and so relieve Paulus at Stalingrad was slowly slipping from his grasp. On 18 December with the cream of his armour burning and his troops fighting to break through what became known as the Aksay Line, the *Feldmarschal* wearily sent a message to General Kurt Zeitzler of the Army High Command requesting that the 6th Army breakout toward 4th Army. However, the appeal was refused.

On 21 December Manstein reported to Hitler that the 4th Panzer Army had advanced within thirty miles from Stalingrad, but the resistance from the enemy was so great that it could make no more progress. There was also no more fuel for the vehicles and without adequate supplies they were doomed to failure. Hitler had been initially encouraged by the success of the 4th Panzer and had ordered the SS-*Panzergrenadier* Division 'Wiking' to be transferred from *Heeresgruppe* A to support the armies' drive to Stalingrad; but it was already too late. With the relief column under threat of encirclement, Manstein had no choice but to retreat back to Kotelnikovo on 29 December, leaving more than 300,000 soldiers encircled in and around Stalingrad to their fate. The limited scope of the Soviet offensive also gave General von Kleist time to withdraw *Heeresgruppe* A out of the Caucasus and back over the Don at Rostov.

With the relief effort in tatters Soviet forces in considerable strength launched a successful offensive against *Heeresgruppe* A. The 1st Panzer Army was quickly withdrawn and evacuated through Rostov in January 1943, before the Soviets could cut it off in the Kuban. On 13 January 1943, four armies of General Golikov's Voronezh Front unleashed a massive attack that encircled and destroyed the Hungarian Second Army near Svoboda on the Don. An attack on the German 2nd Army further north threatened to bring about an encirclement; although the German 2nd Army managed to escape, it was forced to retreat and by 5 February troops of the Voronezh Front were approaching Kursk and Kharkov.

When the last of Field-Marshal Paulus' troops finally surrendered on 2 February 1943 the Red Army found it hard to believe that the battle of Stalingrad had come to an end and that they were victorious. As the gaunt prisoners emerged crawling from the cellars, dugouts, and bunkers, with their hands held high in surrender, the Russians noticed that many of the men had suffered frostbite and could hardly walk. They also observed that the Rumanian soldiers were in a worse shape than their German allies. According to the Rumanians, their meagre rations had been stopped in an attempt to maintain German strength. The loss of life was huge. The Rumanians had lost 173,000 killed, wounded, and missing, of which a quarter had perished through malnutrition and the arctic temperatures. The Croatian expeditionary force had been totally destroyed, including the 369th Regiment which had been wiped out by Russian troops at Stalingrad. The Italians had lost 115,000 dead and wounded, with 66,000 missing, of which a high number probably drowned in the semi-frozen rivers that had cracked open when hundreds retreated across them.

As for the Germans, their losses were equally immense. Some 150,000 Germans were killed, with 91,000 being taken into captivity, many of whom were never to see their homeland again. During the fighting some 30,000 wounded were flown out of the ravaged city.

Russian losses were much higher than those of both the Germans and their allies. Although figures vary, at least 750,000 Red Army troops were killed or wounded. In five months of bitter and bloody fighting, 99 per cent of Stalingrad was destroyed and of the 500,000 inhabitants of the city, only 1,500 remained to endure the horror, with many being caught up and killed in the battle.

Although the Russians had paid a high price in blood for their hard-fought victory, the Germans had lost both an army and a very important campaign. Both the banks of the Don and the Volga were now littered with the dead and the ambitions of the 6th Army had been destroyed. Although Hitler said that the 6th Army had provided a valuable service by tying down almost 750,000 enemy troops, the loss of the campaign was so immense that it marked the turning point of the war in Russia. Never again was Hitler to launch a major offensive in Russia. His army was now faced with a relentlessly growing and improving Red Army.

As German forces of the 6th Army surrendered, all along the German front Army Group A and Army Group Don were struggling to maintain cohesion against stiff enemy attacks. With huge losses and lacking ammunition and equipment to hold back the Soviet forces, German units fell back in confusion all across southern Ukraine. Russian troops now moved forwards in an ambitious operation for the Voronezh Front. Their plan was to advance to the Dnieper and encircle the 2nd Army. The Red Army south-west and southern fronts were to capture Voroshilovgrad and drive south to the Sea of Azov and encircle Kleist's *Heeresgruppe* A and von Manstein's *Heeresgruppe* Don.

The Russia plan went well. Kursk was captured on 8 February 1943, Kharkov on 16 February, and Rostov was abandoned on 18 February. A gap had been driven between *Heeresgruppe* A, which was now being squeezed into a small bridgehead opposite the Kerch peninsula. *Heeresgruppe* Don was also seriously threatened by Kuzetsov's 1st Guards Army which was driving a gap between *Heeresgruppe* Don and von Kluge's *Heeresgruppe Mitte* by advancing through Dnepropetrovsk. However, the problems were made much worse for Manstein when the 6th Army surrendered at Stalingrad on 2 February, releasing Rokossovsky's Don Front for new operations. Despite the best efforts of Manstein to bolster *Heeresgruppe* Don's dwindling ranks, nothing could now mask the fact that they were dwarfed by the superiority of the Red Army.

Intoxicated by its success at Kursk the Soviets attacked *Heeresgruppe Mitte* in the salient at Orel before breaking out towards Bryansk. But despite the German retreat, the Soviets' attack was proving more difficult than they first envisaged. As a consequence the last two weeks of February 1943 saw a tenacious German defence, which consequently saw only minor Russian gains made west of Kursk and none at all at Orel. Yet, despite German resilience, the winter battles had left *Heeresgruppe* Don battered, but still in reasonable shape. Several Panzer units had enough strength to launch a number of counterattacks and Manstein's counteroffensive was stiffened by an SS-*Panzerkorps* equipped with Tiger tanks. On 20 February 1943 it fought its way from Poltava back towards Kharkov, thus gaining the initiative between the Donetz and Dnieper rivers.

By this period of the war, as preparations were made to deliver the stroke against the Soviet Voronezh Front for the battle of Kharkov, *Heeresgruppe* Don was combined with *Heeresgruppe* B and made into the new *Heeresgruppe Süd*. Manstein's counteroffensive that followed was a huge success. It finally ended the Soviet winter offensive, recaptured Kharkov, destroyed the Russian 3rd Tank Army and supporting units, and captured large quantities of equipment between the Donetz and Dnieper.

Manstein had finally restored the *Heeresgruppe*'s position in southern Russia. With renewed confidence German forces of *Heeresgruppe Süd* were being prepared to follow up their success at Kharkov with further bolder attacks east against a huge bulge that now existed in the Kursk sector. What followed in early July 1943 would be the battle of Kursk, which consequently led to the wholesale destruction of German forces in the East.

(*Opposite page*) A German mortar crew during a lull in the fighting on the Eastern Front during the early winter of 1942. They are all wearing the two-piece snowsuit and their steel helmets have received an application of whitewash for extra camouflage protection. The troops who fought in the first winter in Russia made many sacrifices, and those who managed to survive the great ordeal got a medal to prove that they had been there. Troops nicknamed the decoration the 'Frozen Meat Medal', as many of them experienced uncovering the frozen corpses of their dead comrades and giving them proper burials.

German soldiers make the most of the natural environment by constructing a makeshift shelter or igloo in the snow in 1942. Most of the men are wearing the two-piece snowsuit, but there is a soldier who is still without proper white camouflage and can be seen wearing a white snow cloth cover. The use of the white snow cloth cover or blanket was an early attempt by soldiers to camouflage themselves in the snow.

Ski troops move across the snow during winter operations on the Eastern Front in 1942. The troops are wearing the shapeless two-piece snowsuit that consisted of a white jacket and white trousers. To the right of the soldiers is a long column of troops hauling their supplies using a horse and sledge. Movement like this was very risky during daylight hours, as Red Army aircraft regularly attacked German formations out in the open.

(*Opposite above*) Ski troops of the *Gebirgsjäger* during winter operations in Army Group North in 1942. These mountains troops are preparing to move out of a village with sledges full of supplies. The *Gebirgsjäger* were well suited to winter warfare, having been provided with ample supplies of winter clothing. Here the soldiers have been kitted out wearing the familiar two-piece snowsuit. Living in the snow was generally very difficult, but the soldiers were taught that the snow could also serve as an ally, and was not simply an enemy to be feared.

(*Opposite below*) A *Gebirgsjäger* soldier with dogs pulling a sledge across the snow during winter operations on the Eastern Front in 1942. The mountain trooper wears a two-piece snowsuit and is armed with a Kar 98k bolt-action rifle, which has received an application of winter whitewash paint. With the Red Army forces wearing similar winter clothing, front line German troops were normally issued with colour armbands enabling them to distinguish between friend and foe.

Radio operators of the *Gebirgsjäger* using a lightweight radio. These soldiers are probably at a forward observation post, from where they can send details of enemy movements back to divisional headquarters. Both men are wearing the two-piece snowsuit. The white jacket kept the soldiers relatively warm and insulated from the very low temperatures. It was buttoned right up the front with white painted buttons and the garment could easily be removed.

Gebirgsjäger ski troops wearing their distinctive two-piece snowsuit during operations in Russia in 1942. The distances over which the soldiers had to travel were immense. Although these mountain forces sustained heavy casualties during the winter of 1941, they grimly held the line, and by early 1942 a stalemate with the Russians had developed. Before spring only minor skirmishes continued as both sides rebuilt their strength.

German troops wearing the early style greatcoat practising on a makeshift firing range on the Eastern Front with captured Russian Maxim 1910 machine guns. This water-cooled machine gun was mounted on a wheeled Sokolov mount, with its thick armoured shield. Despite its age, it was a very effective weapon, but German troops found that the weapon's fire rate was half that of the MG 34 machine gun.

Gebirgsjäger soldiers are seen here in a forest wearing a variety of winter garments. Many soldiers on the Eastern Front adapted different types of clothing in order to keep warm. The soldier on the right is wearing the two-piece snowsuit, while other soldiers can be seen wearing the single piece snow overall, the standard issue greatcoat with white woollen toque being worn under a Bergmütze, and an animal skin greatcoat. These skin coats varied greatly in size and quality, but they were primarily designed to be worn in extreme cold climates. They were normally worn by officers, but soldiers were also seen wearing them, especially while on guard duties.

(*Opposite above*) Ski troops wearing their two-piece snowsuits advance through a village in 1942. The snowsuit provided good freedom of movement for the troops, especially while skiing. The men are wearing the standard equipment for a rifleman with the usual belt and cartridge pouches, which were generally not camouflaged. The Kar 98k bolt-action rifles that are slung over their backs for ease of carriage have clearly been camouflaged with a coating of winter whitewash paint.

(*Opposite below*) Sheltering in the snow. By 1942 many German soldiers were taught to construct native style shelters from tree branches and to build igloos. These troops, wearing the two-piece snowsuit with the large attached hoods, are erecting an igloo. Beneath the hood they generally wore either the M1935 steel helmet or the Bergmütze.

A *Panzerjäger* crew with their winter camouflaged Pak 38 anti-tank gun on the Eastern Front in 1942. Specially adapted skis have been fitted to the gun wheels and are being transported by animal draught. All the soldiers wear the two-piece snowsuit with the attached hoods over their headgear. Note the variety of equipment worn over the jacket.

(*Opposite page*) A Pak crew in white camouflage smocks can be seen pulling an ordnance through the snow somewhere on the Eastern Front in 1943. By this period of the war the German soldier had learnt to adapt to the harsh arctic conditions of the Soviet Union. They were against an enemy force that had immense toughness and physical strength. The Russian soldier was accustomed to far colder temperatures, which they withstood on far smaller rations than many in the West would have believed possible. Faced with such a foe, the German soldier had to adapt quickly, or die.

Due to the cost, this was one of the least popular winter garments worn by the German Army on the Eastern Front. This was the animal-skin greatcoat with a fur-lined collar. These items of clothing were generally worn by officers in very cold climates. The animal-skin greatcoat varied in both size and colour, and was easily discoloured from continual wear. This soldier is armed with a Kar 98k bolt-action rifle, which has not received any type of camouflage whitewash application.

Gebirgsjäger troops wear the two-piece snowsuit and whitewashed M1935 steel helmets while on the march in northern Russia in 1942. A light 7.5cm infantry gun can also be seen, which has more than likely been towed by horse drawn transport. The authorized strength of a typical mountain division consisted of some sixteen light infantry guns of this type. The most popular weapon used by the *Gebirgsjäger* was the light mountain gun.

Soldiers in 1942 dressed in the familiar winter white reversible. All the men wear special mittens with separate trigger finger, which were normally worn over woollen gloves. They also wear cold weather headdress, which consisted of helmet toques that were a tight fitting camouflage reversible hood and designed to be worn under the steel helmet as part of the reversible winter uniform.

A *Gebirgsjäger* mortar crew preparing to fire their winter-camouflaged weapon during operations on the Eastern Front in 1942. The men are all wearing the two-piece winter suit. Note the soldier on the right with his jacket buttoned-up displaying the metal white buttons. As with all German formations, the mountain troop used the mortar extensively. The weapon was light, easy to carry, and gave the infantryman his own portable light artillery support. But it required training to use; even experienced mortar crews could take several rounds to achieve just one successful hit on target.

(*Opposite above*) A German 10.5cm artillery crew mainly wearing the winter reversible suit with the grey side outer-most. This garment consisted of hooded jacket, trousers and mittens. The material used for the uniform was padded insulating material with water-repellent fabric outer shell. Although specifically worn by the *Waffen*-SS the German Army too did occasionally get to wear them, especially during the later part of the war.

(*Opposite below*) Sheltering out in the snow sometimes proved very difficult. But by 1942 many German soldiers were taught to construct native style shelters from tree branches and to build igloos. These troops, wearing the two-piece snowsuit with the large attached hoods, are erecting an igloo. Beneath the hood they generally wore either the M1935 steel helmet or Bergmütze.

A group of soldiers protect themselves against the bitter night ahead and dig a large foxhole in the snow. The troops are all wearing their 'winter whites', and two of them can be seen with white camouflaged M1935 steel helmets. Of particular interest is the soldier wearing a headpiece made from white cloth material. This was designed to help contain as much body heat as possible and to prevent discomfort from the arctic temperatures while wearing the standard issue steel helmet. Troops often complained that the helmets were like 'freezer boxes' during the winter. Heat loss through the head lowered body temperatures; this led to a very real danger of exposure and hypothermia.

Soldiers of the *Gebirgsjäger* trudge along a road in the rain while operating on the southern sector of the Eastern Front in 1942. The soldiers are all wearing the special waterproof triangle camouflaged cape or Zeltbahn. The Zeltbahn was first issued in 1931 and was carried by each German soldier as part of his personal equipment. The Zeltbahn could be worn as a poncho over the field equipment, and it could also be worn buttoned up under the equipment as a form of camouflage.

A *Gebirgsjäger* soldier wearing the standard pattern field-grey greatcoat with the field-grey collar in the early winter of 1942. Over the greatcoat he wears the black leather infantryman's leather belt with ammunition pouches. An MG 34 machine gun attached to a tripod mounting with an ammunition box can be seen placed strategically at the corner of a busy road junction.

The most universal items of clothing that were worn with the German Army service uniform were the black leather marching boots. The boots were particularly hardwearing and had relatively smooth soles with heel irons. Although they were regarded as comfortable items of clothing, during the winter periods on the Eastern Front the German boot was totally inadequate for wearing in the harsh arctic conditions. The long distances too in which the soldiers travelled also caused the soles to wear down at a considerable rate and as a consequence holes and other parts of the boots' stitching began to fray and open. If not repaired and the cold weather arrived, it was almost certain the wearer would get frost bite.

(*Opposite above*) *Wehrmacht* troops advance forward into action during Operation 'Blau', the German Summer offensive campaign in 1942. Even at this early stage of the offensive it seemed that victory would beckon for the Germans. However, there were still serious concerns that not enough prisoners had been taken and that the 6th Army had got badly strung-out on the 200-mile march. By 25 July the 6th Army had been marching continuously for over two weeks and the men were exhausted, but kept pushing forward because they found that in a number of areas resistance was minimal.

(*Opposite below*) The River Volga has been reached and a cameraman can be seen filming the historic occasion for the propaganda news reels. It was on 23 August 1942 that advanced elements of the 6th Army reached the Volga just north of Stalingrad and managed to capture a strip about five miles long along the river. During their drive east many Soviet troops evacuated their defensive positions in front of the Volga and withdrew into the city.

A quadruple-barrelled self-propelled flak gun complete with crew can be seen out in the steppe during 6th Army's march through southern Russia in late June 1942.

(*Opposite above*) Here soldiers are seen with their injured comrades laying on stretchers preparing to be transported to the rear. By October 1942 casualty rates in and around Stalingrad had risen dramatically. It had been estimated that more than 50,000 German soldiers had been injured in action and few were fit enough to return for front line duties.

(*Opposite below*) German Army tailors working in the field on the Eastern Front in 1942. The army unit tailor with sewing machine is repairing a pair of officer's breeches under a hot Russian sun. The tailor was used widely in the German Army and was normally given duties to repair and adapt various items of clothing. Although the German soldier himself was required to mend his damaged garments with a cotton and thread, officers on the other hand did not need to and passed such tasks over to the unit tailor.

A German unit rests by the side of a road.

Here a group of motorcyclists can be seen outside a workshop. They all wear the standard motorcycle waterproof coat. They also wear around their neck aviator goggles, which were standard issue to all motorcycle units. Motorcyclists could be found in every unit of an infantry and Panzer division, especially during the early part of the war. They were even incorporated in the divisional staffs, which included a motorcycle messenger platoon.

Officers confer with the aid of maps regarding their drive through central Russia. The men wear a variety of shoulder straps and collar patches. For officers who held the rank of *Leutnant* and *Hauptmann* their straps were made of two strands of flat silver braid with red piping, while field officers who held the ranks of Major and above had shoulder straps that consisted of two strands of flat silver with black and green piping.

Gebirgsjäger troops rest and eat before resuming their drive through southern Russia towards the Caucasus Mountains. The *Gebirgsjäger* soldier wearing his mountain cap with the edelweiss badge can clearly be seen wearing one of the many shoulder straps that were introduced into the German Army. The shoulder strap served mainly for displaying the wearer's rank and his branch of service.

Wehrmacht troops advance towards the Volga during Operation 'Blau'. As the Germans stood poised to unleash their forces through southern Russia to the western banks of the Volga, it seemed that the Germans now held the upper hand. At dawn on 28 June 1942, the 2nd and 4th Panzer Armies opened up the 'Blau' offensive. Almost immediately the panzers smashed their way through lines of Red Army defences and drove at breakneck speed east of Kursk and pushed toward Voronezh, reaching the outskirts of the smouldering city in four days. Following the capture of the city the 4th Panzer then swung south-east along the Don where it met with Paulus' 6th Army east of Kharkov. Over the next few weeks, strung out over more than 200 miles, the 6th Army with twenty divisions – 250,000 men, 500 panzers, 7,000 guns and mortars, and 25,000 horses – pushed down towards the Don corridor on Stalingrad.

(*Opposite above*) A group photograph taken of a motorcycle unit. It shows them all wearing their now familiar motorcycle coat with M1935 steel helmet. All motorcycle units and individual motorcyclists, regardless of rank, were issued with the loose-fitting, rubberized coat. The tail of the coat could be gathered in around the wearer's legs and buttoned in position to allow easier movement while on the motorcycle.

(*Opposite below*) Three exhausted soldiers belonging to the *Gebirgsjäger* rest next to a motorcycle combination somewhere in southern Russia in the summer of 1942. Two of the men can be seen wearing the rank chevron indicating that they hold the rank of *Obergefreiter*. The motorcycle sidecar can clearly be seen with a crude painting of the *Gebirgsjäger* edelweiss.

Motorcyclists on exercise. Apart from wearing the motorcycle coat, they are dressed in leather gloves, overshoes and leggings. The gas mask canister, when worn in vehicles or on motorcycles, was for comfort's sake normally slung around the neck instead of across the small of the back. Attached to the motorcycles are the leather saddlebags which contained the cyclist's personal kit and various maps or paperwork.

(*Opposite page*) A soldier on the Eastern Front during Operation 'Blau' in the summer of 1942. This *Unteroffizier* group leader wears the M1936 service uniform with M1935 steel helmet, which by its appearance has been smeared with mud in order to increase the effectiveness of the soldier's overall camouflage. The soldier wears a dispatch case, which is attached to his black leather belt, and on the right an MP 40 magazine pouch can be seen.

A motorcyclist wearing a motorcycle coat, M1935 steel helmet and aviator goggles tests the throttle of his motorcycle under the watchful eye of a field motorcycle mechanic. Riding through the great expanses of Russia, motorcycles were prone to various mechanical faults. As a consequence a well-equipped motorcycle workshop supported the vast number of motorcycles deployed on the Eastern Front, especially in 1941 and 1942.

Motorcyclists have halted on a road in Russia. They wear the motorcycle coat with the M1938 field cap and M1935 steel helmet with aviator goggles. The gas mask canister can be seen slung round on the front of the chest for ease of carriage. In 1940 and 1941 motorcyclists were used extensively for reconnaissance duties. Their very versatile machines enabled them to survey enemy positions until they encountered enemy fire and then return swiftly with important data and other pieces of vital information relating to the location and strength of the enemy.

A commanding officer with the aid of a stick grenade directs a motorcyclist wearing the motorcycle coat. The motorcyclist's primary weapon here is the MP 40 sub-machine gun, which from 1941 was manufactured in great numbers. The usual equipment is worn; of note he wears a pair of MP 39/40 magazine pouches and is also armed with a stick grenade in his right hand. Although a large number of motorcyclists during the early years of the war rode into battle and dismounted to fight, motorcycles and motorcyclists were regarded as vulnerable to small-arms fire and booby traps.

A *Sturmartillerie* enlisted man wears the field-grey jacket with the Death's Head emblem mounted on patches of dark blue-green cloth. He also wears the M1935 steel helmet, which is normally worn under battle conditions. The garment was a very practical piece of clothing, and unlike the black Panzer uniform, it was less conspicuous when the crewman left his vehicle.

(*Opposite above*) September 1942, showing a flak crew during fighting on the steppe. The flak gun is mounted on a halftrack. Both the 2cm and 3.7cm flak gun became the primary light anti-aircraft gun used by the Germans out on the steppe in 1942. However, due to the recurring appearance of heavier enemy armour, flak crews were compelled to divert their attention from the air and support their own infantry and armour on the ground in an anti-tank role. Both weapons are mounted on its cruciform platform and had an effective firing rate of 120 to 280 rounds per minute.

(*Opposite below*) The crew of a StuG.III watch one their comrades flex his muscles during a rest period on the Eastern Front in 1942. These crewmembers wear the normal style field-service army collar patches – normal for personnel below the rank of officer. During the war in Russia, as a temporary security measure the Death's Head emblems were removed from the collar patches of the *Sturmartillerie* and replaced with the normal army field-service collar patches.

A soldier has connected a tow wire to a vehicle in an attempt to try and pull the vehicle out of the mud. The soldier wears the Zeltbahn in order to protect himself from the heavy downpour of rain. There were various methods of wearing the Zeltbahn. It could be used as a poncho for dismounted troops, as in this photograph, and it could also be worn for mounted and bicycle mounted soldiers.

(*Opposite above*) Here the crew of an Sd.Kfz.7 halftrack with a mounted 3.7cm flak gun can all be seen wearing the M1935 steel helmet with Zeltbahn. Early patterns of the Zeltbahn were in field grey, but by 1939 the German Army camouflage splinter pattern was issued to the army. This splinter pattern camouflage was printed in two shades, light and dark, with each side being made from separate pieces of the two types of camouflage cloth.

(*Opposite below*) A group of officers observe their advancing units as they make their way towards the western banks of the Don in August 1942. One of the officers observes the movements through a pair of scissor binoculars.

German soldiers of the 267th Infantry Regiment of the 94th Infantry Division use a deserted Russian farmstead as a defensive position not far from the Volga. A Pak 35/36 can be seen in action. During the battle of Stalingrad the Pak 35/36 was used extensively both against armoured and infantry targets.

German troops, more than likely from the *Gebirgsjäger*, rest on a snow-covered mountainside in Russia in 1942. Behind them sits a captured bullet-riddled bunker that suggests there has been some significant fighting in the area. Both soldiers wear the Zeltbahn. The Zeltbahn was designed with a slit in the middle for the wearer's head and could be worn comfortably over the shoulders hanging down to protect the army field service uniform and field equipment. When worn like this the Zeltbahn was known by the troops as the *Regenmantel* or rain cape.

A *Gebirgsjäger* MG 34 machine gun squad on a mountainside during operations in Russia in 1942. All the troops wear the Zeltbahn. When the wearer no longer required the use of the Zeltbahn it was usually rolled up and fitted to the personal equipment with two leather straps. The Zeltbahn was also sometimes seen attached to the D-rings of the 'Y'-straps, or to the back of the leather belt.

A *Gebirgsjäger* unit is moving along a mountainous road during operations in Russian in 1941. The road is clearly congested with troops, pack animals and various items of equipment and weapons needed to sustain the force during its laborious march. The typical authorized strength of a *Gebirgsjäger* mountain division consisted of some 14,000 troops and 6,000 animals, 4,300 of which were pack animals and 550 mountain horses. All the soldiers are wearing the M1936 service uniform with M1935 steel helmet.

Two *Gebirgsjäger* soldiers can be seen wearing the Zeltbahn. The soldier in the foreground is wearing two Zeltbahn in order to give him even more protection from the rain. The Zeltbahn was designed to be worn around the wearer's body in a number of ways and there had been a wartime army manual produced giving various illustrations as to the method of wear depending on whether the soldier was marching, horse riding, riding a bicycle or just in the field wearing it as a rain cape.

A halftrack towing ordnance in early July 1942. Out in the open dry steppe the dust that the carriages and vehicles frequently threw into the air could easily be identified from a passing aircraft. Quite regularly whole columns were attacked, but the attacks were immediately repulsed by heavy *Luftwaffe* support.

Gebirgsjäger troops with pack animals on the move during operations in southern Russia in 1942. The soldiers are all wearing the familiar service uniform and equipment associated with the *Gebirgsjäger*. It was here in southern Russia that the *Gebirgsjäger* saw extensive action against the Red Army. The previous year they had smashed through the Stalin Line and conducted vigorous attacks deep into enemy territory. They had also participated in the encirclement of the Uman pocket, which saw 100,000 Red Army troops being marched into captivity.

(*Opposite above*) An MG 34 machine gun squad with their commanding officer in 1942. All the squad, except for the officer, who wears the standard army issue greatcoat, are wearing the Zeltbahn. During the last years of the war the manufacturers changed the appearance of the Zeltbahn. It was no longer in two tones, but consisted of just the lighter of the two.

(*Opposite below*) An MG 34 machine gun crew in a defensive position. A well-sighted, well-hidden and well-supplied MG 34 could hold up an entire attacking regiment. This machine gun is perfectly sighted, and could inflict heavy losses on an enemy advance. Inside Stalingrad the MG 34 would prove its worth time and time again.

A soldier can be seen peering through his 6 × 30 binoculars probably on the Eastern Front in the winter 1942/43. He is wearing the reversible padded winter jacket grey side out. This item of clothing was common in both the Army and *Waffen*-SS and was first issued to troops in Russia during the second winter period of the war in late 1942, early 1943.

(*Opposite page*) A German Army chaplain on a podium. All clergy were issued with the standard army service uniform and wore it while following troops in the field, visiting wounded in hospitals, for riding, training, and all official occasions, including preaching to army congregations. On the chaplain's tunic he did not wear any shoulder straps, and the only visible indication of him holding any type of rank were the use of buttons and collar patches. The gold hung crucifix was also part of his uniform and can be seen in this photograph.

An MG 34 machine gunner inside a specially adapted shelter. The machine gunner is wearing the animal skin fur coat with woollen mittens and a toque. The MG 34 was an all-purpose machine gun that could be utilized on the battlefield in both a light and heavy role. It was the most popular machine gun used by the German Army during the war and had a formidable defensive reputation, especially in the later part of the war.

(*Opposite above*) One of the most popular forms of transportation used by the German Army throughout the war were draught animals. Here soldiers can be seen on horseback wearing the Zeltbahn. Occasionally it was not only troops that wore the Zeltbahn, but horses too were seen with the cape draped over the animal, especially during a very heavy downpour of rain or snow.

(*Opposite below*) An Army *Sonderführer* handing out what appears to be official paperwork to civilians. The *Sonderführer* were posted to duties in many areas of administration in the army because of their professional qualifications. In their job they had officer status, but were deemed not to have any official authority in the ranks. Their uniform was very similar to an officer's, but distinguishable by their grey-blue *Waffenfarbe*, simple embroidered patches and shoulder straps. Note the *Gebirgsjäger* officer standing behind the *Sonderführer*.

Officers watch as their men are put through a series of training exercises. The service uniform worn by German Army officers was of higher quality than the normal standard issue army uniform. The officer's service tunic could be worn either with breeches and high riding boots or with trousers and ankle shoes. The officer on the left of the photograph is wearing high riding boots with breeches while the two officers on the right wear ankle shoes and trousers.

Out in the field, two radio operators can be seen inside a foxhole on the Eastern Front in 1942. The soldiers appear to have been here for some time as two Zeltbahn capes have been used as a tent. There were a number of standard designs for constructing Zeltbahn tents, which could house four, eight and even sixteen men. These Zeltbahn tents were ideal rainproof shelters and were used extensively throughout the war, but they were not designed for front line use. They were, however, used for covering the doorways of bunkers.

The soldier standing in the middle is wearing the reversible three-colour splinter camouflage, jacket side out. By late 1942 this item of clothing had become popular in the German Army and worn by all ranks. Note the drawstring attached to the hood of the garment. Because this piece of clothing was reversible drawstrings and buttons located on the camouflage or mouse grey side were duplicated again on the white side.

A soldier is armed with a Kar 98k Mauser bolt action rifle which is balanced over the right shoulder with some of the field equipment attached to the end of the weapon. He wears the Zeltbahn. Each method of wearing the cape ensured that it gave the wearer the maximum amount of protection, while at the same time allowed plenty of movement.

At a command post somewhere in Russia. This photograph shows a variety of uniforms, including the service uniform worn by a General, who can be seen standing at the table. The tunic visibly shows that he has the rank of General. The rank insignia of red and gold collar patches set against a dark blue-green collar with General's style shoulder straps can be seen. Like the officer's tunic, trousers or riding breeches could be worn.

(*Opposite above*) Officers in the field during operations on the Eastern Front in 1942. A well-camouflaged pair of scissor binoculars is being used to survey enemy positions. Three Generals can be seen wearing the familiar tunics with gold collar patches and the silver braid shoulder straps. They also wear the official general officer's service cap.

(*Opposite below*) Infantrymen approaching the Volga in August 1942. The men are examining an empty Russian dugout, which was part of the city's outer defences. During their drive east many Soviet troops evacuated their defensive positions in front of the Volga and withdrew into the city.

In a gully outside Stalingrad a German soldier can be seen asking a captured Soviet soldier questions possibly regarding the location and movement of Russian troop concentrations in and around the city.

(*Opposite above*) German troops push deeper into the city around the factory works. Note the MG 34 machine gun crews hastily employed in the ruins. By early October the 6th Army had suffered huge casualties. Since 13 September it had suffered more than 40,000 killed and wounded. October was ultimately the most important month for the survival of the 6th Army: if it failed to take the city it would be doomed.

(*Opposite below*) A German soldier near the factory works is seen armed with a captured Russian PPSh-41 sub-machine gun. This captured sub-machine gun, nicknamed by the Russians the 'Finka', was widely used by the German Army in Stalingrad. It was rugged, reliable, and had a large magazine capacity.

German soldiers move through a captured part of Stalingrad in September 1942. Though a number of areas in the centre of the city had been captured the Germans were now drawn into a heavy and protracted battle of massive proportions. Soldiers would regularly spend whole days clearing a street, from one end to the other, to prepare for another battle the next day.

(*Opposite above*) An infantry gun crew with their 7.5cm le.IG.18 advancing into Stalingrad. These small light highly mobile infantry guns were more than capable of providing German troops with vital offensive and defensive fire support, particularly when heavier artillery was unavailable.

(*Opposite below*) German troops move forward into action. Many of the buildings in Stalingrad offered the soldiers good cover and provided protection from small arms rounds and fragments.

A mortar crew are seen preparing their 5cm I.Gr.W36 light mortar for action. The I.Gr.W36 fired a small 0.9kg charge to a maximum range of 500m. Though this mortar was used widely in Stalingrad, production of the weapon had in fact been phased out in 1942 due to it lacking sufficient punch.

(*Opposite page*) An interesting photograph showing German aerial reconnaissance pictures of fires raging following heavy *Luftwaffe* attacks on the city's oil storage yard on the Volga, north of the centre of Stalingrad. This photograph not only shows the full extent of the fires but also the size of the city itself.

An MG 34 machine gunner prepares to move forward into action with his unit. In Stalingrad the Germans developed effective defensive tactics and techniques designed around the formidable MG 34 and MG 42 machine gun. In the battles that raged throughout the city, the weapon had considerable staying power.

Out on the steppe near the Volga, captured Russian troops are being marched through a field to a POW compound; their fate can only be imagined.

German armour moving through southern Russian made exceedingly good progress as it advanced towards the Volga. During the march, thousands of Soviet troops were either killed or captured. In this photograph captured Russian soldiers are being transported by halftrack to a POW compound.

An officer converses jovially with his men next to a destroyed Russian tank during early summer operations in Russia in 1942. The officer can be seen wearing his distinctive general officer's service cap along with the high quality tunic and trousers which are tucked into his high leather riding boots.

A 15cm howitzer crew in action against an enemy target. The 15cm field gun was designed to attack targets deeper in the enemy's rear. These included command posts, reserve units, assembly areas, and logistics facilities.

(*Opposite above*) German troops during a fire mission with their 7.5cm le.IG gun. The gun was widely used on the Eastern Front and remained the standard light infantry gun throughout the war. The Germans generally assigned light field guns or pack howitzers to dedicated infantry fire support, though still remaining under artillery control.

(*Opposite below*) In action against a suspected enemy position a halftrack halts with a mounted flak gun in a field. In the distance a farm building burns. This flak gun was fed by 20-round magazines. Apart from its unique anti-aircraft capability it could be used equally well, or even better, against light armoured, soft skin vehicles, field fortifications and fortified buildings. However, in urbanized fighting these vehicles proved to be vulnerable.

An artillery battery's observation post in action. Here the observer peers through his scissor binoculars. Acquiring targets across flat terrain was often much easier than hilly or mountainous terrain. Observation posts were normally located well forward of the infantry they supported, and it was essential that they were well dug in and concealed to ensure battlefield survivability.

(*Opposite above*) A photograph taken the moment a mortar crew go into action against an enemy target. In order to keep the mortar steady and accurate during firing two of the ammunition handlers would hold the tripod. This mortar earned a deadly reputation on the Eastern Front and was used extensively in Stalingrad.

(*Opposite below*) In action is a 15cm howitzer hurling its charge miles into the enemy lines with deadly effect. Although the 15cm howitzer proved a success against enemy targets, by the time Operation 'Blue' was in full swing, gun crews found the weapon too heavy. By 1943 only a few of these guns remained in active service and were used mainly in Russia until the end of the war.

A *Gebirgsjäger* General stands reading some information passed to him by an infantryman. The standard service uniform worn by a *Gebirgsjäger* General was almost identical to the style worn by a German Army General. The General in this photograph wears the piped service tunic with red and gold collar patches. On his right arm he displays the edelweiss arm badge. Instead of wearing the general officer's service cap, he wears the Bergmütze.

Gebirgsjäger soldiers on the side of a mountain during operations on the Eastern Front. While officers converse with their men, who are wearing the standard M1935 steel helmet, a General can be seen approaching them wearing an unbuttoned standard issue greatcoat.

Somewhere in Southern Russia, this picture shows a whitewashed flak gun. Both the 2cm and 3.7cm flak guns became the primary light anti-aircraft guns used by the Germans out on the steppe in 1942. However, due to the recurring appearance of heavier enemy armour it compelled flak crews to divert their attention from the air and support their own infantry and armour on the ground in an anti-tank role. Both weapons had an effective firing rate of 120 to 280 rounds per minute.

An interesting photograph showing a whitewashed 15cm howitzer. Note the wheels have snow chains applied so that the piece could be effectively and quickly employed from one part of the front to another.

The crew of a 15cm s IG33 protect their ears as the artillery gun is fired during an attack against Russian positions in the late winter of 1942. The crew are all wearing white snowsuits and blend well with the local terrain. Life on the front line was terribly hard for the soldiers, especially in sub-zero temperatures. Although the clothing was far superior to that first issued to the men in the first winter, frostbite and hypothermia was still one of the largest causes of battle casualties in the war.

One crewmember can be seen plugging his ears as the whitewashed 15cm howitzer is being fired against an enemy target during winter operations in late 1942.

Gebirgsjäger, or mountain troops, with their pack animals in mountainous terrain on the Eastern Front in 1942. The *Gebirgsjäger* wore the M1936 service uniform, which was similar to that worn by the German Army, except for the edelweiss arm badge worn on the left arm of the tunic, the trousers, the black leather boots, and the mountain troops' field cap or Bergmütze. Here in this photograph the soldiers are wearing the M1935 steel helmet.

Panzerjäger troops with a whitewashed Pak 35/36 anti-tank gun during operations on the Eastern Front in late 1942. All the men wear the newly introduced heavy reversible winter clothing. These items of clothing became very popular during the last three years of the war. Because they kept the soldiers very warm they tended to wear them day and night in cold weather. The soldiers are all wearing the M1938 field cap, which suggests this photograph was taken not under battlefield conditions, but while this Pak crew were training.

Here a German officer can be seen wearing the animal skin greatcoat over his army field service uniform. These garments were very effective at helping to combat the sub-zero temperatures on the Eastern Front. However, like many light coloured items of clothing, they quickly became soiled with dirt.

(*Opposite above*) An artillery crew all wearing toques and the standard army greatcoat can be seen between a 15cm artillery gun on tow and a Volkswagen Type 82 personnel carrier. This photograph was probably taken during the first winter period on the Eastern Front in early 1942. By this time the German Army had experienced its first Russian winter, and virtually the entire front had been brought to a standstill.

(*Opposite below*) A German infantryman guards Russian prisoners as they are marched through the snow. The German soldier wears the winter white reversible, which is caked in mud. It was quite common to see the winter reversible discoloured with dirt and filth, especially after continual use of the garment. Troops found it almost impossible to wash these suits and as a consequence combat soldiers were supplied with a thin cotton cape or cover that could be worn over all the uniform and equipment. This was easier to clean.

Chapter Three

Winter and Spring Campaign 1943

While German forces on the southern Front were fighting for survival, in the north the Red Army went on the offensive on 18 January 1943 in order to try smashing the siege of Leningrad and driving back the forces of German Army Group North. Although the Soviet attack went well the German defensive positions were too strong. By the summer of 1943, the front continued to hold. German strength in July was 710,000 men, and Army Group North was also building up a huge number of reserves, echeloned in depth behind the northern fronts in Estonia and Latvia. The Germans and Soviets in northern Russia were almost equal in strength, but the Red Army was known to have substantial reserves. They were also building up significant forces to weaken German defensive positions around Leningrad and Nevel. However, by the end of 1943 the army's tactical position had become very fragile. This was made worse on 14 January 1944 when the Red Army launched its winter offensive against the Leningrad and Volkhov Fronts. The German 18th Army was outnumbered by at least 3:1 in divisions, 3:1 in artillery, and 6:1 in tanks, self-propelled artillery, and aircraft. By the morning of 18 January the fronts east of Oranienbaum and west of Leningrad were collapsing. The same was happening at Novgorod where a number of German units were being encircled. The Russian 2nd Shock and 42nd Armies then joined the attack against Army Group North. Along the Baltic coast some German elements escaped, but many were trapped and destroyed as the Russians swept in from the east and west. At Novgorod eight Soviet divisions encircled five German battalions. Their one hope was to escape annihilation by hiding in the swamps west of the city. As Novgorod was pulverized into oblivion by heavy Russian artillery, the 42nd Army attacked toward Krasnogvardeysk and started battering German units defending the town. The 18th Army was beginning to dis-integrate. Fighting in mud and swampland, the troops were exhausted. On 23 January Pushkin and Slutsk were evacuated. General Kuechler, the new commander of *Heeresgruppe Nord*, appealed to Hitler for a complete withdrawal. Hitler responded angrily and prohibited all voluntary withdrawals, reserving all decisions to withdraw to himself. However, one week later, after the 18th Army had incurred more than

50,000 casualties, Hitler approved a retreat to the Luga River but directed that the front be held, contact with 16th Army regained, and all gaps in the front closed.

From their positions, soldiers of the 16th Army watched anxiously as the Russians began increasing their attacks. Commanders in the field were well aware that if the hold on Leningrad were broken, Army Group North would eventually lose control of the Baltic Sea, Finland would be isolated, supplies of iron ore from Sweden would be in danger, and the U-boat training programme would be seriously curtailed. It was now imperative that the troops hold the front and wage a static battle of attrition until other parts of the Russian front could be stabilized. The Germans tried their best to hold the lines by shifting *Luftwaffe* field divisions and SS units newly recruited in the Baltic States to help prop up weak *Wehrmacht* units.

Elsewhere along the German front, depleted forces tried in vain to bolster their dwindling troops. While many parts of the front remained stagnated, in the south and in the Ukraine, the campaign was being decided. By late February 1943 the front had moved almost 200 miles in less than three months. As the German soldiers withdrew they devastated wide areas of countryside and razed towns and villages to the ground. But despite the German slow retreat, it was in essence a tactical withdrawal. The Soviets themselves found the fighting more difficult than first envisaged, and were quite aware that the war in the East was far from finished.

During the last two weeks of February a complete dramatic reversal of fortune gripped the German Army, which was later called by the soldiers that fought in it, 'the miracle of the Donetz'. South of Kharkov under converging pressure from General Hoth's two Panzer Corps, the exhausted Russian armies began to disintegrate and retreat in an easterly direction. In early March German pincers had closed following a meeting between Hoth's forces and the *Waffen*-SS. However, due to their relatively small numbers German infantry were unable to seal the pocket completely, allowing many relieved Russian troops to claw their way out of the cauldron on foot or horseback and limp back to their lines battered and bruised, crossing unguarded parts of the frozen Donetz. Despite the escape of thousands of Soviet soldiers, German forces finally found themselves on almost exactly the same line from which they had first set out the previous winter. The German Army had yet again demonstrated its renowned powers of recovery.

Intoxicated by their success on the Donetz, soldiers recaptured the blitzed city of Kharkov, and plans were immediately drawn up for a massive attack on the Kursk salient. Although the German Army had successfully stabilized the Eastern Front, its soldiers had no longer the strength to mount another successful offensive like those seen in 1941 and 1942. Nevertheless Hitler, emboldened by the success of the German Army, tried once more to take the initiative in the East, gambling everything he could muster at Kursk. The Germans were poised in the summer of 1943 to either gain the initiative, or to be driven into a long, painful and bitter retreat.

Two StuG.IIIs move through the snow while operating on the Eastern Front during the early winter of 1943. One practical item worn by Panzer, tank destroyer, and self-propelled assault gun units was the German Army issue winter reversible, seen here being worn white side out. However, armoured crews soon found that the winter side was easily soiled with dirt, oil and grease.

A group of soldiers pose for the camera somewhere in Russia during the late winter of 1942, early 1943. They all wear the new reversible winter uniform, which was first introduced on the Eastern Front during this period. The garment was designed large enough to be worn over the German army field service uniform including the basic field equipment. However, the majority of soldiers preferred wearing their equipment over the winter jacket. Although the winter reversible was a popular item of clothing it soon became very dirty from constant wear and defeated the objective of the white camouflage.

A photograph showing the effects of a flamethrower hitting a target.

A machine gunner armed with an MG 34 machine in a defensive position. The barrel of the gun is being protected from the extreme freezing temperatures. Despite the terrors of the Russian winter, in which the Red Army often had considerable advantage, the Wehrmacht were determined not to be beaten. Instead of retreating across the drifting snowfields, with the possibility of being annihilated by the enemy, the men fought it out, waiting for the spring thaw.

Three *Panzergrenadiers* during the winter of 1943 are wearing a variety of clothing and personal equipment. Two of the soldiers wear the German Army greatcoat while the other man wears a white camouflaged cape over the great-coat. The cape was also worn over the winter reversible suit in order to protect it from dirt on the battlefield.

The crew of a Pz.Kpfw.IV pose for the camera before the men resume operations on the Eastern Front. The Pz.Kpfw.IV became the most popular Panzer in the *Panzerwaffe* and remained in production throughout the war. Originally the Pz.Kpfw.IV was designed as an infantry support tank, but soon proved to be so versatile and effective that it earned a unique offensive and defensive role on the battlefield.

A Panzer crew pose for the camera on board their Pz.Kpfw.IV in 1943. A typical five-man crew comprised of the driver, radio-operator, machine gunner, loader and commander. The crew is wearing the denim Panzer working and summer vehicle uniform. These garments were considerably lighter and made life inside the baking hot compartment of the tank more bearable than the thick woollen black Panzer uniform.

A Panzer crew belonging to Panzer Regiment 6 of the 3rd Panzer Division are seen here wearing a variety of winter clothing over their standard black Panzer uniform during the late winter of 1943. The commander is the only crew-member wearing his black Panzer uniform but with a scarf and a fur pile cap. The Panzer man behind the commander wears an animal skin fur coat with sleeves removed and a white fur M1943 field cap. The other two crewmembers are dressed in army reversible anoraks.

A group of *Wehrmacht* troops rest beside an armoured vehicle during operations in the spring of 1943. The men are equipped with various items of kit including the gas mask cape and rifle ammunition pouches for their Karabiner 98K rifle. Note the commander wearing an M35 dispatch case with an MP 40 slung over his shoulder.

Two troops wearing the green splinter pattern Army camouflage smock with fur caps. There were two styles of the jacket made, the splinter green and the mouse-grey camouflage version. Both were reversible items of clothing. No type of insignia or badges other than rank insignia was worn with this type of clothing.

A crewman poses for the camera next to his StuG.III. Ausf.G in the summer of 1943. The *Panzerjäger Obergefreiter* wears the special field-grey uniform worn by crews of tank destroyer and self-propelled assault gun units. The style of the uniform was very similar to that of the black Panzer uniform, but this special garment was made entirely of field-grey cloth. The collar patches too differed between those crews of different types of military units who were entitled to wear the uniform. This crewmember wears the Death's Head emblem mounted on patches of dark blue-green cloth and edged with bright red *Waffenfarbe* piping.

A *Wehrmacht* soldier can be seen armed with a Karabiner 98K bolt action rifle. This rifle was the most universal rifle in the German Army. It was reliable, robust, light, and effective.

Next to a destroyed building, a 7.5cm le.IG.18 light infantry gun can be seen here in action. This weapon could not only be fired quickly and accurately but also had an advantage on the battlefield by having a low profile design and splinter shield.

Two photographs taken in sequence showing a well concealed soldier, probably belonging to an artillery battery, at a forward observation post. He can be seen looking through his well camouflaged 6 × 30 Sf.14z scissors binoculars, which are mounted on a high tripod. These binoculars were nicknamed 'Eselsohren' – donkey ears.

German troops take cover alongside a building during operations in the spring of 1943 somewhere on the Eastern Front. By this period of the war enemy resistance was stiffening and German casualty rates were rising.

(*Opposite above*) A Panzer crew rest in a field during the summer months. One crewmember can be seen drinking water from his canteen. In 1943 the Pz.Kpfw.IV played a prominent role in a desperate attempt to halt the Soviet onslaught. Even though these powerful tanks were vastly outnumbered it was ultimately a credit to the Panzer divisions it served.

(*Opposite below*) A German position near the River Don in 1943. Troops have made good use of the local terrain and built shelters into the sides of the gully. Tents and other shelters have also been erected. A 15cm howitzer can be seen in the background in an elevated position.

A photograph of a typical *Wehrmacht* soldier wearing his tunic and M1938 field cap in the spring of 1943.

(*Opposite page*) At a mobile field post, an officer can be seen making notes and adjustments to his map during operations on the Eastern Front in the spring of 1943.

A photograph taken of a well-dug-in 8cm GrW34 mortar complete with two-man crew. This weapon was the principle infantry mortar used by both the *Wehrmacht* and *Waffen*-SS. Six were normally assigned to an infantry battalion's machine gun company.

A mortar crew. By 1943 the German front lines were now badly scarred and depleted, and along some sectors of the front its forces no longer had sufficient supplies or manpower to contain its positions for any appreciable length of time. German troops were battered and bruised from months of ceaseless combat and were desperately trying to hold their positions.

A dirty-faced German soldier poses for the camera during his march. During the dry summer months in southern Russia the sand and dust was a constant problem for the soldiers. Not only did the particles sift into engine motors and the interior of tanks and other vehicles, but soldiers inhaled it too. Handkerchiefs and other forms of protection were used around the mouth and nose, but this did not prevent the soldier becoming covered with dust.

A flak gun mounted on the back of a halftrack towing a single axle trailer negotiates an uneven piece of terrain. These vehicles were used widely used against both ground and aerial targets. With the folded down sides the gun was very adaptable and could traverse 360 degrees, making it a lethal weapon of war.

An interesting photograph showing two quadruple-barrelled self-propelled anti-aircraft guns mounted on halftracks. By 1943, mechanized formations were well equipped with flak guns. There were motorized flak battalions, with divisions being furnished with additional anti-aircraft platoons and companies in the *Panzergrenadier*, Panzer and artillery regiments. This gun was a formidable weapon and was more than capable of combating both low flying aircraft and ground targets.

(*Opposite above*) A PaK35/36 anti-tank gun can be seen readied for action. Foliage has been applied to the gun's splinted shield to break up the weapons distinctive shape.

(*Opposite below*) Troops can be seen trying to relieve a vehicle stuck in mud. Interestingly, Soviet POWs can be seen helping. By 1943 German commanders had become very much aware of how roads could vanish in just a few hours of rain, and how, two years into the campaign in Russia, they were heavily dependent on the few all-weather roads that had been built in western Russia.

Due to the appalling road conditions the use of the main roads was restricted generally to priority class vehicles such as tanks and halftracks. Next in priority came the ammunition columns and fuel convoys, and then the reinforcements needed to nourish the advance. The nearer to the battle zones, the worse the road system became. Here in this photograph a staff car has become stuck in the mud.

A member of a motorcycle unit poses for a photograph. With his standard M1936 tunic he wears standard aviator goggles. The motorcycle was used for both combat and reconnaissance roles.

(*Opposite page*) An MG 34 machine gun, mounted on a Dreifuss 34 anti-aircraft tripod mount, has been erected on a river bank guarding the pontoon bridge, which is allowing the movement of draught animals and supplies to cross unhindered.

Four soldiers can be seen near a dugout. These men are probably attached to a forward observation post.

German troops can be seen resting beside a road during the early summer of 1943. The soldiers had to march immense distances and the exhaustion of fighting continuously from one part of the battle front to another often took its toll on the men.

Boats have been pressed into service by assault troops. Two paddles either side was normally sufficient for the boats to be propelled through the water, even when loaded with a full complement of infantry with heavy weapons and equipment.

Soldiers can be seen moving to another position during the early summer of 1943. Both men at the front have stick grenades at the ready. Behind them is a heavy MG 34 machine gun crew.

A knocked out Soviet tank and an abandoned Russian artillery piece. While the Russians were slowly taking the initiative in the first half of 1943 the Germans were as determined as ever to fight on doggedly and cause as much damage as possible to the Soviet lines.

A column of troops, passing heavy road traffic, march to the front caked in the dust of the sandy roads whipped up by the harsh Soviet steppe winds.

A smiling German soldier can be seen wearing an M1936 tunic and cravat. The cravat was probably used to prevent dust particles getting into his mouth while on horseback.

A *Wehrmacht* soldier rests. The arduous days marching and fighting were exhausting for the men and they often slept wherever they could.

German troops can be seen marching along a dusty road watched by the local inhabitants. By 1943 the Germans were slowly withdrawing through the Ukraine, but doggedly fighting in some areas as they tactically withdrew.

Troops can be seen withdrawing to another line of defence across a wooden bridge.

Russian troops surrender and raise their arms. Strangely they can be seen smiling to their captors. The smiling was probably more to show the Germans that they had surrendered in peace, inwardly concerned about their impending fate.

Near a river a *Wehrmacht* unit has halted, poised before resuming its march again. The photograph looks normal, but to the right, near the stationary Horch Cross Country vehicle, is a movie camera set up on a tripod. This probably indicates that this is a staged area, especially arranged for the propaganda news reels.

Appendix I

Assessment of the German Soldier 1941–1943

When the German soldier ventured out across into Russia when 'Barbarossa' was first unleashed, the Red Army was a complete enigma to him. There was little information supplied about the country which he was invading, nor was there anything substantial on the terrain and climate. He simply saw the Russians as Slavic people of an inferior race. Propaganda had proved conclusively that all Russians were living in poverty and its antiquated army was totally unprepared for war. Even when the German soldier rolled across into Russia during the summer months of 1941, he was unaware of the immense undertaking he had before him if he was to crush the enemy.

Although the ordinary German found a huge contrast between his own country and that in which he was fighting, he was unprepared for the unimaginable size and distances which he would have to march. The soldiers were amazed by the immense forests, the huge expanses of marshland, and the many rivers that were continuously prone to flooding. They were also surprised to find that the little information they did have, was often incorrect. Maps frequently showed none of the roads, and when they were fortunate enough to come across them, they were in such a terrible state of repair that military traffic would often reduce them to nothing more than mud tracks.

Another great contrast that the German soldier experienced during his march through Russia was the climatic conditions. There were extreme differences in temperature, with the bitter cold sometimes dropping to 30 or even 40 degrees below zero, and the terrible heat of the summer when temperatures soared to insufferable levels. When the first snow showers arrived, in October 1941, the German soldier was unprepared for a Russian winter. Sleet and cold driving rain turned the Russian countryside into a quagmire, with roads and fields becoming virtually impassable. The lack of winter clothing caused widespread worry for the soldiers for they knew that the winter would create graver problems than the Russians themselves. By late 1941 supplies of winter clothing began arriving at the front, but many soldiers did not receive their garments until the first half of 1942. In an attempt to restore morale among the soldiers, which had been lost due to the harsh winter conditions of 1941/2, the army produced a winter warfare handbook. This book was primarily designed to assure the German soldier that he could deal with the arctic conditions, and a special chapter was written dealing with clothing and food. During 1942 various items of clothing were designed and introduced to help combat the Russian climate and increase the survivability of the German soldier on the battlefield.

Throughout 1942 the German soldier slowly adapted to the Russian climate and terrain, and was seen wearing a host of new summer and winter camouflage uniforms, and newly designed steel helmets and field caps. Even the Panzer uniforms were being replaced. But despite the drastic measures implemented in the design of better uniforms and equipment in order to sustain the German soldier on the battlefield, nothing could mask the fact that they were up against an enemy that were numerically superior and fiercely contested every foot of ground to the death. To make matters worse the terrain also heavily influenced the conduct of military operations, especially for the German soldier of the 6th Army as he marched across seemingly unending expanses of flat terrain, sometimes encountering bitter opposition along the way. In the south the Germans had the greater area to clear. Although the vast steppes were regarded as good tank country they lacked drinking water, and many soldiers suffered as a result. Yet despite the hardships that each man encountered he was determined to fulfil his duty, reach the river Volga, and capture a little known city called Stalingrad.

Personal Equipment & Weapons

The German soldier was very well equipped and perhaps in 1939, when the German war was unleashed against Europe, they were the best equipped in the world. The rifleman or *Schütze* wore the trademark mode 11935 steel helmet, which provided ample protection while marching to the battlefront and during combat. His leather belt with support straps carried two sets of three ammunition pouches for a total of sixty rounds for his carbine. The soldier also wore his combat harness for his mess kit and special camouflage rain cape or Zeltbahn. He carried an entrenching tool, and attached to the entrenching tool carrier was the bayonet, a bread bag for rations, gas mask canister (which was invariably slung over the wearer's shoulder) and an anti-gas cape in its pouch attached to the shoulder strap. The infantryman's flashlight was normally attached to the tunic and inside the tunic pocket he carried wound dressings. A small backpack was issued to the soldiers, though some did not wear them. The backpack was intended for spare clothing, personal items, and additional rations along with a spare clothing satchel.

The weapons used by the German soldier varied, but the standard issue piece of equipment was the 7.92mm Kar 98k carbine. This excellent modern and effective bolt-action rifle was of Mauser design. It remained the most popular weapon used by the German Army throughout the war. Another weapon much used by the German Army, but not to the extent of the Kar 98k, was the 9mm MP 38 or MP 40 machine pistol. This sub-machine gun was undoubtedly one of the most effective weapons ever produced for the German war machine. The 7.92mm MG 34 light machine gun was another weapon that featured heavily within the ranks of the German Army. The weapon was the most effective machine gun ever produced at that time. The MG 34 and later the MG 42 possessed a very impressive fire rate and could dominate the battlefield both in defensive and offensive roles. The German Army issued the MG 34 to every rifle group, and machine gun crews were able to transport this relatively light weapon easily onto the battlefield by resting it over the shoulder. Yet another weapon, which was seen at both company and battalion level on the battlefield, was the 5cm l.GrW36 light mortar and 8cm s. GrW34 heavy mortar. Although they could both be an effective weapon when fired accurately the light and heavy mortar was far too heavy and too expensive to produce on a very large scale.

At regimental and divisional level the German Army possessed its own artillery in the form of 7.5cm l.IG18, 10.5cm l.FH18, 15cm s.FH18, and 15cm s.IG33 infantry guns. Specially trained artillery crews used these guns and they were seen extensively in Poland, Western Front, Balkans, and the first two years of war in Russia. The 3.7cm Pak 35/36 was another weapon that was very popular especially during the early years of the war. However, by the time the German invasion of Russia was unleashed *Panzerjäger* crews soon became aware of the tactical limitations of the weapon.

Appendix II

German Infantry

The German *Heer*, or army, was formed in May 1935 following the reintroduction of military conscription. Within three years of the carefully controlled conscription programme the Army had built up a formidable fighting force, both in men and formations. In the German Army the arm of service consisted of heavy infantry, light (*Schützen*) units, security (*Sicherungs*) or police detachments, and various other types of light infantry (*Jäger*) formations.

For the coming war the German army was trained to play a very specific role on the battlefield, and was well tailored to carry out that role quickly and decisively. It was considered by its commanders to be the paramount arm of the service and for this reason it grew rapidly in strength, so much in fact that during the Second World War the German Army fielded some 700 infantry divisions. These divisions were numbered serially from 1 to 719, but were made more complicated by the inclusion of some divisions that were named instead of numbered, by deliberate gaps left in sequence, and by other types of infantry units that had their own numbering system. Later during the war certain divisions were retitled as *Volksgrenadier*, which was a description given by the Nazi Party in their belief that by bestowing distinctive names to a division, that would imbue the soldiers of that division to fight on to the bitter end.

Although many formations were included in the infantry divisions or under Army command, divisions like the Jäger and the mountain troops (*Gebirgsjäger*) were outside the numbering system of the standard infantry divisions, as were the *Luftwaffe* and the *Waffen*-SS. The Panzer Divisions, which were commanded by the Army, also had their own separate numbering system.

At the start of the war the battle line thus included the standard infantry divisions, and these men had first been conscripted in 'waves' or 'classes' of men. Initially the infantry divisions were numbered 1 to 36 and 44 to 46 and were the regular divisions. The second wave consisted of divisions numbered 50 to 100; the third wave composed of waves 200 to 250; and the fourth wave 251 to 300. The series 501 to 600 was left open without filling them with divisions in order to raise new formations. Late in the war these empty numbers were filled with *Volksgrenadier* units and the infantry numbering system was well over 700. During the last years of the war there had been a massive influx of other units accepted into the infantry divisional serial numbering system, which included the *Panzergrenadier*, *Panzerjäger*, fortress, field training, static motorized, *Gebirgsjäger* and *Luftwaffe* divisions.

Standard German Infantry Division

With the onset of war in 1939 the German infantry division had changed little from the assault divisions of 1918. The bulk of its supply and transport units were still by animal draught. The standard infantry rifle had basically not been changed since the war in the trenches, but its machine guns, notably the MG 34 and mortars, were far superior to anything the enemy could muster. The artillery had changed little except that of the 10.5cm field howitzer, which had replaced the 7.7cm 18 infantry gun. Communication too was vastly superior to that of the enemy.

The Infantry division in 1939–41 averaged 16,860 men. This was made up of the following:

Officers	518
NCOs	2,573
Other Ranks	13,667
Officials	102

Of the total standard infantry division, only about 65 per cent consisted of combat troops, the remainder were support elements of the division.

Three infantry regiments comprised:

Officers	75
NCOs	493
Other Ranks	2,474
Officials	7

(Also included were staff and intelligence units)

Reconnaissance (*Aufklärungs*) Battalion	623 officers and men
Anti-tank (*Panzerjäger*) Battalion	550 officers and men
Engineer (*Pionier*) Battalion	520 officers and men
Artillery (*Artillerie*) Regiment	2,872 officers and men
Light (*Leichte*) infantry 'column'	30 men
Signal (*Nachrichten*) Battalion	474 officers and men
Supply services (*Versrgungsdienste*)	226 officers and men
Logistics column/supply train (3 motorized, 3 horse drawn)	180 officers and men
Petrol, oil and lubricants column	35 officers and men
Workshop Company	102 officers and men
Transport Company	245 officers and men
Veterinary company	235 officers and men, and 890 horses

2 Medical companies   616 Officers and men
   (1 Field Hospital and 2 medical
   transport platoons)

The infantry divisions also included the rations platoon, Bakery Company, butcher platoon, Military Police, and feldpost.

Typical German Infantry Division Prior to 1943

	Motor Vehicles	Horse Drawn Vehicles
Divisional headquarters (including administration, supply, medical, police, postal, and veterinary units)	253	245
Signal Battalion	103	7
Reconnaissance Battalion	30	3
Artillery Regiment	105	229
Anti-Tank Battalion	114	0
Engineer Battalion	87	19
Three infantry regiments: 3,250 men each, and each with 683 horses, 6 small infantry guns, 2 large infantry guns, and 12 anti-tank guns	75 ($\times$ 3)	210 ($\times$ 3)
Total Strength	911 (17,000 men)	1,133 (5,375 horses)

Appendix III

6th Army Order of Battle
19 November 1942

6th Army was destroyed at Stalingrad 31 Jan 1943 and was reformed Mar 1943

Commanders

Generalfeldmarschall Walter von Reichenau	(20 Oct 1939 – 1 Jan 1942)
Generalfeldmarschall Friedrich Paulus	(1 Jan 1942 – 31 Jan 1943)
Generaloberst Karl Hollidt	(5 Mar 1943 – 22 Nov 1943)
General der Artillerie Maximilian de Angelis	(22 Nov 1943 – 19 Dec 1943)
Generaloberst Karl Hollidt	(19 Dec 1943 – 8 Apr 1944)
General der Artillerie Maximilian de Angelis	(8 Apr 1944 – 17 July 1944)
General der Artillerie Maximilian Fretter-Pico	(17 July 1944 – 22 Dec 1944)
General der Panzertruppen Hermann Balck	(23 Dec 1944 – 8 May 1945)

Order of battle (19 Nov 1942)

HQ
IV Corps
   29th (Mot.) Infantry Division
   297th Infantry Division
   371st Infantry Division
VII Corps
   76th Infantry Division
   113th Infantry Division
XI Corps
   44th Infantry Division
   376th Infantry Division
   384th Infantry Division
XIV Panzer Corps
   3rd (Mot.) Infantry Division

60th (Mot.) Infantry Division
16th Panzer Division
LI Corps
71st Infantry Division
79th Infantry Division
94th Infantry Division
100th Jäger Division
295th Infantry Division
305th Infantry Division
389th Infantry Division
14th Panzer Division
24th Panzer Division
9th Flak Division
51st, 53rd Mortar Regiment
2nd, 30th Nebelwerfer Regiment
4th, 46th, 64th, 70th Artillery Regiment
54th, 616th, 627th, 849th Artillery Battalion
49th, 101st, 733rd Heavy-artillery Battalion
6th, 41st Pioneer Battalion

Appendix IV

Rank Equivalents

German Army	Waffen-SS	British Army
Gemeiner, Landser	Schütze	Private
	Oberschütze	
Grenadier	Sturmmann	Lance Corporal
Obergrenadier		
Gefreiter	Rottenführer	Corporal
Obergefreiter	Unterscharführer	
Stabsgefreiter		
Unteroffizier	Scharführer	Sergeant
Unterfeldwebel	Oberscharführer	Colour Sergeant
Feldwebel		
Oberfeldwebel	Hauptscharführer	Sergeant Major
Stabsfeldwebel	Hauptbereitschaftsleiter	
	Sturmscharführer	Warrant Officer
Leutnant	Untersturmführer	Second Lieutenant
Oberleutnant	Obersturmführer	First Lieutenant
Hauptmann	Hauptsturmführer	Captain
Major	Sturmbannführer	Major
Oberstleutnant	Obersturmbannführer	Lieutenant Colonel
Oberst	Standartenführer	Colonel
	Oberführer	Brigadier General
Generalmajor	Brigadeführer	Major General
Generalleutnant	Gruppenführer	Lieutenant General
General	Obergruppenführer	General
Generaloberst	Oberstgruppenführer	
Generalfeldmarschall	Reichsführer-SS	

Notes